WINGS
ON THE RIVER

FLYING BOATS ON
THE BRISBANE RIVER & REDLAND BAY

DAVID JONES

National Library of Australia
Cataloguing-in-Publication entry:

Jones, David (David Embry), 1945- .
Wings on the river : flying boats on the Brisbane River and
Redland Bay

1st ed.
ISBN 9781921054273 (pbk.).

1. Seaplanes - Queensland - Brisbane River - History. 2.
Seaplanes - Queensland - Redland Bay - History. 3.
Seaplanes Queensland - History. 4. Air travel -
Australia - History. 5. Aeronautics - Australia - History.
I. Title.

387.73347

Typeset by Boolarong Press, Salisbury, Australia.

Printed and bound by Watson Ferguson & Company, Salisbury, Australia.

Wings on the River

Flying Boats on the Brisbane River and Redland Bay

David Jones

Contents

Table of Maps

Cover picture: Qantas Short S.23 Empire flying boat *Cooee* over the Brisbane River on 3 May 1938 with the incomplete span of the Story Bridge below. (Photo courtesy of Sutcliffe Gallery Australia, www.sutcliffegallery.com.au)

Foreword

By George A. Roberts OAM,

On Short Brothers Empire 'C' Class S23 Flying Boat, Forerunner of the Short Sunderland S25 of World War Two Fame

For a passenger engaged in travel on an Empire flying boat, the romance of its 9½ day flight from Australia to the United Kingdom, flying over or setting down on the waters of many and various countries en-route, differed greatly from that of the previous land 'plane service.

Commencing July 1938 on a schedule reduced from 12½ days, the through service by each aircraft was operated jointly by Qantas Empire Airways and Imperial Airways, with a crew change at Singapore, later Karachi, the result of World War Two interference and the closing to traffic through the Mediterranean Sea.

Unlike the land 'plane, with cabin provision for ten and a crew of two, which from commencement at Archerfield, Brisbane, followed an inland route and towns through Queensland and the Northern Territory to Darwin, the flying boat service, based at Rose Bay, Sydney, flew a coastal course, refueling on the Brisbane River and at Gladstone for its first night stop at Townsville.

Qantas's Short Empire flying boat *Cooee* arrives over the centre of Brisbane city on 3 May 1938. (QEA postcard via George Roberts)

On departure the following morning, breakfast on board, it touched down at Karumba and Groote Eylandt in the Gulf of Carpentaria for its second night stop at Darwin.

With a technical crew comprising Captain, First Officer and Radio Officer stationed on the aircraft's upper, separated flight deck of the all metal, four engine monoplane and equipped with auto-pilot, passengers were seated in three spacious cabins, each with a table, a galley and meals served by a Flight Steward.

At their disposal, a promenade deck, large windows and supporting handrail, assisted by the parasol effect of the aircraft's wing, gave passengers access to viewing of the passing scene below, while all mail in large amounts was carried in the forward cabin.

Initially speculative of the these operations amounting to three services per week in each direction, the residents of Rose Bay were soon entranced by the comings and goings of these big birds, their manoeuvring when released from the mooring buoy, as under power the hull rose onto the step, planed, then broke away from the water's surface tension. As seen from the people's balconies and windows, gaining height, the aircraft circled around the rising terrain of Point Piper, Bellevue Hill, Dover Heights and Vaucluse, or alternately, on alighting, the keel cut the water like a knife.

History records a departure from Darwin, across the Timor Sea to Koepang, Singapore and beyond, when a young First Officer on his inaugural flight was questioned about his future, he remarked "to see another land"!

In my capacity as a Qantas aircraft engineer, my duties included many, many flying hours in each of the Empire flying boats (32 in number) and to alight on the waters of my home State, Brisbane, also to experience the romance of these operations, embedded in my memory these thoughts return as though it were yesterday.

Geo. A. Roberts

George A Roberts OAM

Acknowledgements

In compiling this history I am grateful for the generous input and support provided by many people. I am particularly indebted to George Roberts, OAM, of the Qantas Heritage Collection, whose immense knowledge of flying boats covers the full time span of this book, and who has so kindly graced this book with a foreword. I am also indebted to Frank Kelly, inaugural pilot with Barrier Reef Airways, who has unparalleled experience of flying boat operations in Queensland. Both these distinguished veterans willingly shared their wide range of memories and information with me, kindly answering my many questions, and assisting me in every way possible.

Special thanks are due to flying boat historian John Wilson for generously making his accumulated local knowledge and photo collection available to me and for checking the accuracy of my text. My thanks also go to Mrs. Marion Eaton, who grew up in the Whitsundays, for sharing her own historical information with me and opening doors which furthered my research.

I appreciate also the support given to me by members of the Sunderland Branch of the RAAF Association, Queensland Division, for welcoming me into their family and sharing their experiences in the special world of flying boats. In particular I acknowledge the assistance of Jack Kennedy and Len Roberts who, as Sunderland pilots, flew through Hamilton during the war.

My thanks go to all who had contact with Brisbane's flying boat past and shared their experiences with me. These include my uncle, Eric Jones, whose career with DCA touched on Brisbane's flying boats and who enthusiastically supported my research throughout; Graeme Gillies, whose father had a distinguished career as a flying boat captain in war and peace; Tom Nunan, who passed on his memories of flying boat travel out of Redland Bay; and Redland Bay residents Graham Barnett, Tom Bland, Doug Lindsay and John Moore. I am deeply grateful to Ian Beasley, Merlean Black, Robert Blaikie, Ian Hall and Ron Peterson who very kindly made copies of their photos available to me and for sharing their memories of these aircraft.

I am also grateful to historians who have generously assisted with information and contacts. These include Jim McPherson and Peter Nunan of the Queensland Maritime Museum, Ron Cuskelly and David Bussey of the Queensland Air Museum, Tracey Ryan of Cleveland Library local history room, Moreton Bay historian Peter Ludlow, and World War Two historians Roger Marks and Russell Miller.

A work of this type depends heavily for its completeness and accuracy on archival records. In this regard I express my appreciation for their assistance to the staff of the National Archives of Australia at Brisbane, Canberra and Melbourne and of the Queensland State Archives.

Last, but by no means least, I want to recognize the very strong contribution my family has made to the completion of this book. Firstly I warmly thank my wife, Heather, for her faith in me and patience throughout the life of this project, and for the interest and support of my children, Rhonwen and Bradley. I also acknowledge with gratitude the part played by my late father, Mervyn Jones, who passed on to me his lifelong love of aircraft. It was his passion, as he photographed flying boats on the river in the 1920s and 30s that was the genesis of this book.

David Jones
Brisbane, 2007

Hawker Osprey reconnaissance seaplane from the cruiser HMS *Sussex* floats lightly on the South Brisbane Reach of the River late in 1934; a handy photo opportunity for my father during a lunch hour in the city. (Mervyn Jones)

Introduction

"There's something about Flying Boats that produces an atmosphere amongst men even more satisfactory than flying land planes. Possibly it arises from coping with two rebellious elements, the sea and the air."[1]

These reflections by "Scotty" Allen, arguably Australia's leading flying boat captain, capture the romantic appeal these aircraft had for all who knew them. Few would remain unmoved when they saw a big flying boat blasting through the waves in a burst of sound and spray as it strove to rise free of the sea and into the air. It is a sight that has receded well into the past and, as air services become faster and more competitive, is unlikely to return.

Yet, during the first fifty years of air travel, flying boats represented comfort and safety in reaching distant and exotic places across the sea. Between the two World Wars, Brisbane saw seaplanes mooring in the heart of the city. They linked Brisbane initially with Britain and later with the USA during the course of World War Two. Then following the War, the wings of flying boats returned and the Brisbane River became home to a flying boat airline serving the Great Barrier Reef.

But there were risks for seaplanes on the river, and in 1953 Brisbane's water airport moved to the quiet safety of Redland Bay. Regular flying boat services faded away soon afterwards. But Redland Bay stayed operational for two decades, little used, but available in case of emergency by aircraft on the Sydney – Lord Howe Island route: the last flying boat airline service in the world.

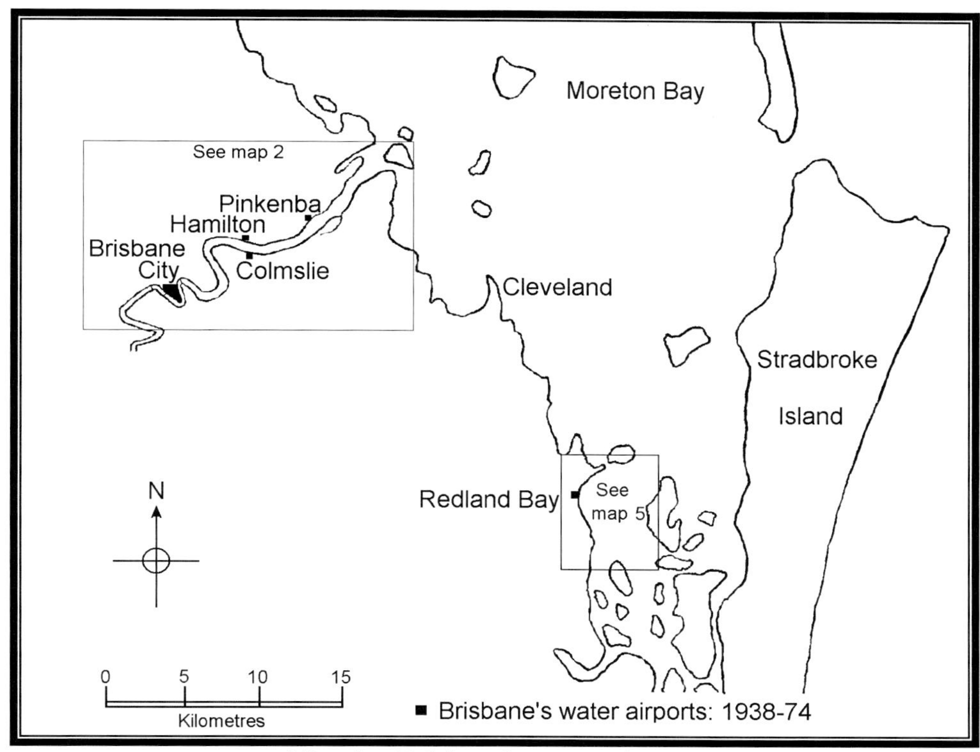

Map 1 – Brisbane's water airports

Chapter 1 – Pioneers and Goodwill Visitors

"As we flew up the wide waters of the [river] I could not help thinking how practical was our method of flying, for beneath us was one long, continuous landing-ground."[1]

After the First World War ended, returning airmen sought to introduce Australia to the new world of aviation and its exciting possibilities. But their flying remained limited by weather and the existence of sufficiently large and flat areas of cleared ground to land or take off. Free from this last restriction were seaplanes which could travel widely as long as there was a stretch of clear, relatively calm water available. Brisbane, with its broad river passing through the city and Moreton Bay close by, was well suited for use by seaplanes.

A pioneer of seaplanes in Australia was Lebbeus Hordern, son of the Sydney retailer. Early in 1920 he imported a pair of Curtiss Seagull flying boats, and one of these soon came north to conduct an aerial survey in New Guinea, selecting suitable refuelling stops en-route. George Roberts, then only ten years old but later to have a distinguished career with Qantas, was given a joy-flight in this aircraft while on holiday at Sandgate.[2]

H.C. "Horrie" Miller took over the Seagulls to introduce a regular service between Adelaide and towns on the South Australian gulfs. This scheme did not succeed and he moved to Queensland. In December 1924 he brought one of the Seagulls to Brisbane, and after assembly at Hamilton, he used it for joy-flights at Southport. He found the sheltered bay waters ideal and it was a successful season for the battling airman.[3] Miller would later make his mark on Australian aviation as founder of MacRobertson Miller Aviation which secured the air mail contract for Western Australia and the Northern Territory in 1934. MMA continued as the foremost regional airline in the area for another fifty years.

As aviation struggled to gain acceptance in the post-war period, a far-sighted RAAF officer, Wing Commander S.J. Goble, obtained his Minister's approval for an ambitious project to circumnavigate the Australian continent by air. As well as demonstrating the capability of the fledgling RAAF, the flight had a strategic purpose in blazing a trail for seaplanes to fly up Australia's east coast from the RAAF's main base at Point Cook in Victoria to Thursday Island. It would also trial air operations in tropical conditions.

Leaving Point Cook early on 6 April 1924 with Flight Lieutenant I.E. McIntyre in a Fairey IIID twin float seaplane, Goble was in Sydney next day. Continuing north the flyers encountered constant rain, enforcing a 24 hour delay at Port Stephens. Resuming their flight on 9th they alighted on the Broadwater at

Southport at 5.10pm where a large crowd, as well as supplies of fuel awaited them on the foreshore. Goble and McIntyre bypassed Brisbane as they hurried north to Gladstone.[4] From Thursday Island they crossed the Gulf of Carpentaria in a single stage. Continuing around Australia's remote northern, western and southern shores they reached Melbourne again on 19th May, having become the first aircraft to fly right around Australia's coastline. They had covered almost 13,800km in twenty days of flying. For this fine achievement Goble and McIntyre were presented with the Britannia Challenge Trophy, awarded in Great Britain for the most meritorious flight of the year.[5]

Just over a year later, on 1 June 1925, another seaplane touched down at Point Cook after an international flight of equal distinction to that of Goble and McIntyre. Major the Marquis De Pinedo and his mechanic E. Campanelli departed from Brindisi in Italy on 27 April 1925 in their single engine Savoia S.16 flying boat. Theirs was only the third aircraft to complete the flight between Europe and Australia. After making their landfall at Broome, they proceeded south along the Western Australian coast and eastwards across the Great Australian Bight.[6]

De Pinedo and Campinelli taxi their Savoia flying boat to the Naval Stores at Kangaroo Point on 6 August 1925. (State Library of Queensland, neg no. 65540)

Their aircraft was overhauled at Point Cook, then De Pinedo turned northwards and made an overnight call at Brisbane on Thursday 6 August 1925. The Savoia arrived over Brisbane just before 2pm at the end of a four hour flight from Sydney. It had been a fast passage and De Pinedo arrived an hour early. He made a wide circuit of the city, alighted off the Botanic Gardens and taxied to moorings at the Naval Stores at Kangaroo Point.[7]

The Savoia had covered 25,750km without mishap by the time it reached Brisbane, but there was a long way still to go. On the following morning De Pinedo took off at 8am for Rockhampton on the next stage of his journey to Tokyo via New Guinea, the East Indies, the Philippines, China and Korea. After visiting Japan, De Pinedo and Campanelli flew their aircraft home to Italy in only 22 days.[8] It was a magnificent achievement, being the first return flight between Europe and Australia. Including their visit to the Far East, they had travelled over 56,000km in a flight free from major incident.[9]

The year of 1928 was one of spectacular achievements by the pioneers of Australian aviation. In February Bert Hinkler was the first pilot to fly solo from England to Australia, making the journey in just over half the time of any previous aircraft. What made his flight all the more sensational was that his aircraft was small, with an engine of only 85hp. Hinkler's magnificent feat was matched on 8th June when Charles Kingsford Smith and his crew landed the *Southern Cross* in Brisbane at the end of the first air crossing of the Pacific Ocean.

A week before the *Southern Cross* touched down at Eagle Farm a formation of Royal Air Force flying boats alighted on the opposite coast of Australia making their own contribution to aviation progress. The formation consisted of four Supermarine Southampton II flying boats which were among the largest aircraft then in service with the RAF. Named the Far East Flight under the command of Group Captain H.M. Cave-Browne-Cave, these aircraft were sent from Great Britain for service based in Singapore. But before they became permanently established they would complete an extended cruise of the Far East and Australia. The cruise was intended to demonstrate the mobility of aerial forces over long distances, and give valuable experience of unsupported operations.[10]

When the four Southamptons arrived at Broome on 1 June 1928, only six aircraft had completed the flight from Europe to Australia before them. Furthermore, theirs was the first successful flight to Australia by a group of aircraft and it demonstrated the RAF's professionalism in sustained long distance flying. The flying boats cruised around the western and southern coastlines of Australia, staying for a month at the RAAF base at Point Cook followed by ten days in Sydney.[11]

Continuing their journey northwards, the aircraft made an impressive arrival in Brisbane at 1pm on Saturday 11 August 1928. The press reported these "giants of the air" circled in "George Cross" formation over the city, passing over the Brisbane Exhibition Ground where the RNA Show was then in progress. Then they landed off the Gardens to be "greeted by the sirens of numerous river craft and the cheers of onlookers on the river banks."[12] The Southamptons stayed in Brisbane for a week, attracting considerable attention as they rested off the Domain in the heart of the city. Early on the following Saturday morning they taxied upstream to take off from Milton Reach.

Their northerly course up the Queensland coast took them to landings at Gladstone, Bowen, Cooktown and Thursday Island. The flying boats finally left Australia on 1 September bound for Koepang and Singapore.[13] In the three months they had been in this country they had circled the continent and called at 21 ports. The Far East Flight continued their tour to Hong Kong before finally settling down at their new base in December 1928, 14 months after leaving Great Britain. The four flying boats had performed impressively throughout their long cruise, covering 43,500km free from mishap.[14]

****

Alighting and mooring as they did in the city centre, brought flying boats prominently into the public eye and their pioneering and goodwill flights had a powerful impact on the people of Brisbane. The RAAF's own seaplanes called from time to time as also did occasional visiting aircraft. The RAAF obtained nine Supermarine Seagull III amphibians and a pair of Southampton I flying boats in the late 1920s and both types gave ten years good service to the nation. The Seagulls carried out an aerial survey of the Great Barrier Reef based in Bowen between 1926 and 1928 before embarking on HMAS *Albatross*, Australia's first aircraft carrier, in 1929.

But facilities to assist seaplanes on the Brisbane River were minimal in the period between the wars. In September 1934 the RAAF laid a line of mooring buoys in the South Brisbane Reach of the river off the Domain, where Parliament House and the QUT now stand. These were coated with rubber to minimise damage to flying boat hulls and the area was designated an official airport.[15]

But no other special provisions were made for seaplanes. If repairs were needed their crews were directed to the airport facilities at Archerfield and cranes available at commercial wharves in the Town Reach. Pilots were advised that stretches of the river over a mile (1.6km) long were available in all directions for landing and taking off, but alighting near the Domain where they were close to the RAAF moorings was recommended.[16] Most of the biplane flying boats, with their built in headwinds of struts and wires, had no difficulty landing here, approaching over Victoria Bridge into the south-easterly breeze and coming to rest on the 750 metre stretch of water downstream from the bridge.

RAAF Supermarine Seagull III amphibian moored off the Domain with South Brisbane Town Hall and Somerville House beyond. (Mervyn Jones)

Taking off was a different matter as a loaded flying boat needed a much longer distance to gain sufficient speed to overcome the water's drag and lift into the air. The four RAF Southamptons moved upstream to take off from lengthy Milton Reach, but after the Grey Street (now the William Jolly) Bridge was completed in 1932, visiting flying boats preferred to move downstream to take off, using either Bulimba or Hamilton Reach. This involved a long taxi down the river made difficult by the river's sharp bends which placed the wind successively behind and ahead of the aircraft. Not only did this cause handling difficulties, but engines were prone to overheat on a long run and in a following wind.[17]

It was possible for some light seaplanes to take off from South Brisbane Reach. After being unloaded on nearby wharves on 6 March 1936 a Fairchild amphibian used by the Archbold natural history expedition was flown out to Archerfield.[18] In October 1938 a Short Scion twin engine float plane arrived in Brisbane to introduce daily flights from the Domain Reach of the river to the Southport Broadwater and Tweed Heads. But due to damage received on the water and recurring engine trouble this aircraft received little use and was subsequently put up for sale.[19]

****

The 1930s saw two more goodwill flights by formations of RAF flying boats which repeated the spectacle of the Far East Flight's earlier visit. The first of these took place in October 1934 when three Short Rangoon flying boats represented the RAF at celebrations for Melbourne's centenary. The Rangoons were larger and more powerful than any aircraft previously seen in Australia and their roomy cabins contained bunks and a galley enabling up to seven crew members to be fully self-sufficient on board.[20] The formation, commanded by Group Captain R.E. Saul, was drawn from 203 Squadron based in Iraq and reached Darwin on 27 September 1934.

One of three majestic Short Rangoon flying boats that visited Brisbane during October 1934. The flour mill survived into the 1980s when it was removed to make way for World Expo 88 on South Bank. (Mervyn Jones)

Continuing around the northern Australian coast, the Rangoons were due to arrive in Brisbane at 3pm on Tuesday 2nd October after an overnight stay at Bowen and a refuelling stop in Gladstone. However the big flying boats found themselves butting into strong south-easterly headwinds throughout the day and were two hours late reaching Brisbane. Their spectacular arrival was observed by large crowds as they alighted over the Victoria Bridge in the South Brisbane Reach of the river.[21]

The Rangoons remained in Brisbane for three days, moored off the Domain where they attracted considerable interest from city workers and sightseers. Their all-metal, fully enclosed hulls were the first seen in Australia, and seeing three aircraft of such size together made a strong impression. They left Brisbane early on 5th, taxiing eleven kilometres downstream to Hamilton Reach before finding a sufficiently long stretch of water to enable them to take off. They completed their journey in Melbourne three days later. Throughout their flight the three flying boats maintained their planned timetable, arriving at each port of call on the day originally scheduled. It had been a creditable performance.[22]

However, while in Melbourne the Rangoons' accomplishments were overshadowed by the Centenary Air Race from London to Melbourne. The race winner completed the course in just under three days, and two of the new all metal airliners entering service in the USA finished only a day later. These achievements considerably escalated the standards and expectations of world aviation.

Four years after Melbourne's festivities, there were further celebrations for Australia's sesqui-centenary – the 150th anniversary of European settlement in Australia. The main celebrations centred on Sydney harbour during the week of Australia Day 1938. Bonds of Empire were strong and the RAF was represented at the occasion by a flight of five Saro Londons, their standard patrol flying boat of the time. These twin engine biplanes belonged to 204 Squadron (Wing Commander K.B. Lloyd) and their cruise would be the longest formation flight made by the RAF up to that time. For the trip the Londons were fitted with a large long-range fuel tank which more than doubled their range.[23]

The flying boats' journey was difficult, departing from Plymouth on 1 December 1937 in a howling, winter gale and the poor weather stayed with them across Europe and the Mediterranean. Crossing the Equator they entered the southern tropical monsoon season, battling through torrential downpours and cyclonic conditions as they progressed across the Dutch East Indies and northern Australia.

Despite their difficulties, the flying boats maintained their schedule and were expected to arrive in Brisbane between 11am and noon on Friday 21 January 1938. As lunchtime approached, hundreds waited with picnic lunches on the riverbank to greet the Londons' arrival, while water police cleared the river of obstructions.

Around noon, the flying boats appeared in formation over the city. Gliding in over the cliffs at the southern end of South Brisbane Reach they alighted on the river at two minute intervals and taxied back to their buoys off the Domain. Their arrival had lived up to expectations both as a spectacle and in its timing. The five immaculate aircraft made an impressive sight. Never before and never again would Brisbane see so many large flying boats moored together in the heart of the city, behind Parliament House.[24]

On Tuesday morning, 25th January, the five Londons taxied down to Bulimba Reach of the river to take off in succession. But their departure did not proceed smoothly. Half way down Bulimba Reach the old paddle-steamer *Hetherington* operated a car ferry service between Commercial Road, Newstead, and Oxford Street, Bulimba. As the five flying boats lined up to take off the *Hetherington* continued to ply her trade, crawling across the river and causing several aircraft to abort their run.[25] Bulimba was clearly unsuitable for further use by flying boats.

Designed to an Australian order, the Supermarine Seagull V, seen aboard HMAS *Hobart* on the Brisbane River in August 1939, became the highly successful Walrus of World War Two. (Mervyn Jones)

The RAF flying boats remained in Sydney throughout the anniversary celebrations then moved on to Point Cook for several weeks of rest and overhaul. The five aircraft returned home in May 1938 having been away for six months and covering 48,000km.[26] Like their RAF predecessors it was a professional performance, emphasising again the reliability and safety of flying boats for long distance travel.

But the biplane Londons belonged to a passing era. Preceding them into Brisbane and sharing the celebrations on Sydney harbour was another British flying boat, so much more advanced that the Londons appeared antique in comparison. This was *Centaurus*, the first of a new generation of large, monoplane flying boats that would revolutionise international air travel to Australia.

Chapter 2 – Flying Boats to Great Britain

"Today we can write 'Dear George' at the beginning of a letter and feel assured that George will be reading it less than 10 days later 12,000 miles away."[1]

Centaurus was the outcome of a radical change in policy by the British Government three years earlier. In the mid 1930s, the British aviation industry was being pressed on two sides – by demands for providing faster and cheaper air mail services across the Empire; and by competition from speedy, modern airliners being built in the USA. Drastic change was needed on Britain's air routes around the globe.

First step in answering this challenge was a decision by the British Government at the end of 1934 that in future, all mails throughout the Empire would be carried by air. To meet this requirement, Short Brothers of Belfast designed the S.23 Empire flying boat, which was capable of carrying heavy volumes of mail rapidly over long distances. The S.23 was a large, four engine monoplane of all metal construction, as up to date as any being built overseas. The design showed such promise that Imperial Airways decided to use this flying boat on all its Empire air routes and ordered 28 off the drawing-board.[2] As the airline's "C-class", all would carry a name commencing with the letter "C".

Longest of all the Empire air routes was that between England and Australia. Regular services along the route were introduced in 1934 by Imperial Airways with Qantas operating the Sydney to Singapore sector. The airliner used by Qantas was the de Havilland biplane DH86. Built of wood and fabric, the DH86 was typical of the outmoded designs that were causing Great Britain to fall behind in the air. The fine new Empire flying boats represented a massive advance in technology, comfort and capacity over the DH86. The Short Empires were fitted with new instruments such as the automatic pilot, and unprecedented comfort including a promenade saloon with a 2.75 metre ceiling.

With a much greater payload, the flying boats were expected to make a strong impact on the Empire air route and by the middle of 1938 they had replaced the older aircraft currently in service. Qantas would continue to partner Imperial Airways and six Short Empires were ordered for the Australian airline.

But the British decision was not well received by the Commonwealth Government. Their policies favoured land based aviation and they objected to the extra cost involved and what they saw as British interference. Before the flying boat scheme could be implemented refuelling sites needed to be identified along the whole route between Sydney and Singapore. Then within Australia, alighting areas had to be surveyed and terminals built with adequate facilities for servicing these large, new aircraft and their passengers. This would take time, particularly for the more isolated refuelling stops in northern Australia.[3]

A survey of the route between Singapore and Sydney was arranged by Qantas and Imperial Airways with experts from the RAAF and the Civil Aviation Board joining them for the Australian sector. Using a RAF Short Singapore III flying boat, approaching the size of the new Short Empires but of traditional biplane design, the party left Singapore on 7 May 1936. They advanced through the Netherlands East Indies and northern Australia before proceeding down the east coast to Sydney.

The Singapore was slow and sluggish in climbing, and Hudson Fysh commented "it was not an aircraft to inspire."[4] Its arrival in Queensland coincided with a period of boisterous weather which slowed its progress considerably and disrupted interstate air services. After reaching Brisbane on Wednesday 20th May, the big flying boat remained for five days. Continuing south on 24th, it was forced back by the weather but succeeded in completing the journey next day.[5]

Opinions of those participating in the survey were divided. In Brisbane Qantas's Hudson Fysh recommended Hamilton Reach but the RAAF's Squadron Leader A.E. Hempel said the Brisbane River was specially deficient in the characteristics desired.[6] Ultimately Pinkenba was agreed upon and surveys and planning were able to proceed. Other Australian ports selected for the new flying boat service were Darwin, Groote Eylandt, Karumba, Townsville, Gladstone and Sydney.

Meanwhile on 4 July 1936, the Short Empire flying boat made its maiden flight with complete success. The new aircraft was on track to transform long distance travel around the British Empire in speed, comfort, and reliability. In January 1937 Empire flying boats commenced services in the Mediterranean and by the middle of the year they were flying regularly from Britain to South Africa and between New York and Bermuda. On the route to Australia the new flying boats took over operations to Karachi in October 1937, extending these to Calcutta in the following February. It was only a matter of time before they reached Australia.

After all the promise and anticipation, the first Short Empire flying boat arrived in Australia in December 1937. The aircraft was *Centaurus*, commanded by Captain J.W. Burgess, who had captained one of the RAF Rangoons that had visited Australia three years earlier. *Centaurus*'s visit fulfilled a range of objectives, foremost of which was proving the practicalities of operating Empire flying boats over the complete air route to Australia. Planning by Imperial

Airways and Qantas was well advanced for the introduction of this service, but their plans did not stop there. *Centaurus* would pass beyond Australia to New Zealand as a precursor to extending the Empire Air Route there in the near future.

The shape of things to come – *Centaurus* lies in the heart of Brisbane during her exciting visit to Australia and New Zealand in December 1937. (Mervyn Jones)

Her visit would be a major promotional occasion, both for its promise of improving air services to England, and for restoring faith in British aircraft design. The brand new aircraft would also fly the flag of the British aircraft industry at Australia's sesqui-centenary celebrations in January 1938.

After covering 21,000km in 18 days, *Centaurus* reached Brisbane on Tuesday 21 December 1937. The big, streamlined aircraft did not attempt to land in the city as previous flying boats had done, but chose the longer Bulimba Reach instead. With Qantas flight superintendent Captain Lester Brain at the controls, *Centaurus* taxied eight kilometres upstream to its moorings off the Domain.[7]

Centaurus was by far the largest and most advanced aircraft seen in Australia up to that time and she attracted much attention from the press and the public. The new generation of all-metal American airliners had arrived in Australia within the previous twelve to eighteen months, overshadowing the wood and fabric construction that had been standard up to that time. The latest of these, the Douglas DC3, had just entered service in time for the Christmas traffic in 1937.[8] However, with its size and unprecedented luxury, the Short Empire flying boat was clearly in a class of its own.

Sightseers went to see *Centaurus* at her moorings off the Domain and large articles and photos of her appeared in the newspapers each day. One of the many sightseers was Robert Blaikie, then a small boy. Almost seventy years later he clearly remembers walking with his uncle and grandfather through the long wet grass to a spot on the river bank near the flying boat. This fine aircraft made such an impression that a framed photo of her taken by his uncle that day is displayed in his home.[9]

While many came to admire, no demonstration flights were undertaken while she was in Brisbane. Nevertheless there were authorities to impress, and 180 dignitaries visited *Centaurus* during her stay.[10] Early on Christmas Eve *Centaurus* left her moorings and taxied downstream to Bulimba Reach to take off for Sydney. She carried a full load of passengers including press reporters and several Qantas officials and aircrew.

Christmas was spent in Sydney, but early on Monday 27 December she set off on the first flying boat crossing of the Tasman Sea and the final stage of the first through flying boat flight from Great Britain to New Zealand. *Centaurus* would be in the air for nine hours before arriving at Auckland. She spent two weeks in New Zealand visiting Auckland, Wellington, Lyttelton and Dunedin before returning to Sydney in time for Australia's sesqui-centenary celebrations.

The festivities over, *Centaurus* called again at Brisbane on 27 January 1938 on her return journey. This time she alighted at Pinkenba, but soon took off again with 17 guests for a short flight over the city. *Centaurus* then taxied upriver to the city where the flying boat's engines would be overhauled by Qantas ground staff.[11] Three weeks later, Captain Burgess brought *Centaurus* safely back to Southampton Water after a round trip of 55,300km. The big flying boat had performed beautifully throughout.

****

Following *Centaurus*'s visit, the arrival of the first of Australia's own Empire flying boats was awaited with enthusiasm. The portents were good as Brisbane was headquarters of Qantas Empire Airways and the new flying boat would be spending several weeks working up air and ground crews on Brisbane River. Even the name of the new aircraft, *Coolangatta*, was propitious as it came from the local area.

Coolangatta left Southampton on its delivery flight to Australia on 18 March 1938 commanded by Captain G.U. "Scotty" Allen, who had been flying Short Empires with Imperial Airways for the past three months. The new Australian flying boat ran the established service to Singapore, then continued on to reach Darwin on Wednesday 30th March.[12] At 12.30pm on 2nd April *Coolangatta* arrived over Brisbane and Captain Allen brought her down to a gentle landing on the river at Pinkenba to be met by a small party of official guests.[13]

Australia' first Short Empire flying boat, *Coolangatta*, touches down at Pinkenba on 2 April 1938. (GCCC Local Studies Library; LS-LSP-CD105-IMG0094, Lionel Perry photographer)

Next day, Sunday 3rd, an estimated 2,500 people with 500 motor cars made the trip to Pinkenba to see Australia's first, world-class flying boat. But they were disappointed. Instead of *Coolangatta* being available for public viewing, she was anchored some distance away off Meeandah Reserve. Launches were warned off by a watchman to prevent the expensive flying boat from being damaged.[14] It was an unhappy introduction for the people of Brisbane. But for Qantas it was a major step forward in their progress as an international airline. A month later on 3rd May, *Coolangatta* was joined by her sister *Cooee* flown by Captain P.W. Lynch-Blosse, which had made the flight from England in ten days.[15] Scheduled services were due to commence in only two months time, and there was much to be done before Qantas would be ready to meet that day.

The site chosen for introducing regular flying boat services through Brisbane was at Pinkenba. Here the river was broad, with long uninterrupted reaches, and free of the cross-river traffic that created a hazard in the built up areas. Surrounding land was low allowing loaded aircraft to take off and alight with ease and safety.

Centaurus trialled the use of Pinkenba during her return to England. Work had already started on dredging the offshore area for flying boats and continued through the following months as Brisbane's flying boat terminal was built. Qantas proudly announced that no facility for efficient working of the new service would be lacking.[16]

Two mooring buoys were laid immediately upstream from Pinkenba Railway Wharf and an area 366 metres long by up to 91 metres wide was reserved as a flying boat anchorage.[17] Buildings were leased from the Railway Department and converted to offices for Qantas and Civil Aviation staff, and quarters were fitted out for mechanics. A pontoon was installed beside the western end of the wharf for embarking and landing passengers who travelled to and from their flying boat by launch. Facilities for refuelling and servicing aircraft from lighters were established, and moorings installed for service launches. Finally a windsock was erected over the offices to show that this truly was an airport.[18]

The advent of scheduled airline services prompted the authorities to implement rules governing their movements in harbour. Regulations for controlling aircraft in harbours were drafted in 1937 by the Commonwealth in consultation with the States and these were adopted under Queensland's "Air Navigation Act 1937". Among other things these stated that "after alighting [seaplanes] become, for all practical purposes, motor vessels and in manoeuvring must conform with Harbour Regulations."[19] Support launches were required to be in attendance ensuring the area was clear of obstructions, and they stood by at take offs and landings. The free and easy days for flying boats on the river were over.

Prior to 1937 all of Qantas's aircraft had been land based, and converting to seaplanes required a significant change in culture. Ground staff had to be trained in servicing flying boats over water and a marine section was needed to provide small boat support.

But most important of all, pilots needed to learn new skills for handling flying boats on the water. One flying boat pilot described this as an art in itself – every take off was different. Once engines were started, the flying boat began to move and moorings were slipped immediately. The aircraft was then subject to wind, tide and wave conditions. The strength and direction of the wind required careful handling of engines and rudder for manoeuvring and a stiff breeze would find the flying boat swinging into it like a weathercock. A choppy sea was always dangerous requiring split second timing by the pilot. A crash could easily result if the nose dug into a wave on take off or if a landing was too heavy.[20]

The Saro Cutty Sark amphibian later used for training by Qantas taxies ashore during joy-riding at Suttons Beach, Redcliffe. (State Library of Queensland, neg no. 160550)

To prepare its pilots for these changes Qantas purchased a Saro Cutty Sark four seat amphibian which had been touring Queensland as far north as Townsville testing the market for tourist flights and giving joy rides. While normally based at Archerfield, the Cutty Sark would enable Qantas crews to practice water landings, take offs and handling on the river at Pinkenba in preparation for the Empire flying boats' arrival.

The small amphibian provided useful training until on 5 April 1938 it came to grief in a landing accident. In attempting to alight at Pinkenba the amphibian somersaulted as it touched the water and came to a stop on its back. The three crew members scrambled to safety while their aircraft remained afloat due to the buoyancy of its wing. The Cutty Sark's crew had neglected to retract the amphibian's undercarriage after leaving Archerfield and its wheels were still down when they attempted to alight on the river. The aircraft's back was broken during salvage operations and it was written off as a total loss.[21]

This did not greatly affect the training programme as Qantas's first Empire flying boat, *Coolangatta*, had arrived in Brisbane three days earlier. She gave air and ground crews realistic experience and when *Cooee* joined her sister at Pinkenba the pace of training increased.

But training at Pinkenba was only temporary as the terminus of the Empire air mail service was moving beyond Brisbane to Sydney. Qantas Empire Airways shifted its head office from Brisbane to Sydney over the weekend of 28-29 May 1938 and the two flying boats followed a fortnight later on 10th June.[22]

There was plenty of work ahead of them in their new home. The new flying boat base at Rose Bay on Sydney harbour was far from finished. The contract for erecting a hangar had not yet been let and contract terms allowed 30 weeks before completion was required. Until the hangar and landing ramp were built there were no effective facilities for servicing flying boats south of Singapore.[23]

****

Despite delays in building seaplane bases, the date for commencing services was set as Tuesday 5 July 1938. For the first month it was regarded as a "running-in service" with mails being off-loaded at Darwin and transferred to Qantas's existing DH86 service for carriage to Brisbane. Once the running-in period was over three services a week would operate in each direction. These would arrive in Brisbane from Great Britain at 12.15pm on Monday, Tuesday and Saturday each week, and depart for the return service to Southampton at 11am on a Tuesday, Thursday and Saturday.[24] The full journey between Southampton and Sydney was scheduled to take 9½ days, cutting 2½ days off the current schedule. Stop-over times in Brisbane were 40 or 45 minutes with flight times to the next port being 3 hours 20 minutes southbound to Sydney and 4 hours to Gladstone.[25]

The flying boat's 16 passengers were carried in unprecedented comfort with full-length reclining seats, a steward providing cabin service, and for the first time hot meals were served in flight. But the £200 price of a ticket to England was exclusive, representing a year's wages for the average working man.[26]

In accordance with arrangements, the first outgoing flying boat to England left Sydney at 7am on 5 July 1938. Piloted by Captain Lynch-Blosse, *Cooee* arrived at Brisbane's fresh, new water airport at 10.15am met by a small group of spectators. Ground staff refuelling and loading *Cooee* were still gaining experience and her turn-around took half an hour longer than scheduled. Continuing their journey north, *Cooee*'s passengers were served a three course lunch on the way to Gladstone. They finished the day in Townsville where they spent the night.

Qantas's second Short Empire, *Cooee*, arrives over Brisbane for the first time on 3 May 1938. The tallest office buildings in Adelaide, Queen and Elizabeth Streets below are only ten storeys high. (*Courier Mail* photo via John Wilson)

The reciprocal service from England was also due in Brisbane on the 5th flown by Imperial Airways' *Challenger*. She left Southampton on 28 June 1938 under the command of Qantas's most experienced flying boat pilot, Captain "Scotty" Allen. But *Challenger* struck trouble in her northern Australian ports. The flying boat arrived in Darwin after dark in boisterous weather and several of her passengers became seasick waiting to be taken ashore. Later *Challenger* was struck by a fuel barge which delayed her 24 hours.

5 July 1938 not only raised the curtain on the Short Empires, but also introduced their competition. Prior to this, Qantas was the sole operator of international flights into Australia, but the Dutch airline KLM had been pressing to extend its service between the Netherlands and the East Indies into Australia. KLM was equipped with the new generation of fast American airliners and sought reciprocal landing rights in Australia for those provided to Qantas in the Netherlands East Indies.

After a route proving flight to Sydney in June, KLM's East Indies subsidiary KNILM was ready to commence services with modern Lockheed 14 Super

Electras. KNILM offered two return flights a week to Batavia linking with KLM services to Holland. The total passage of eight days from Sydney to Amsterdam meant travellers could reach England a day earlier with the Dutch airlines than they could in the Empire flying boats.[27]

Tuesday 5 July 1938 was a record day for aviation in Brisbane. As *Cooee* was taking off at Pinkenba, Super Electra PK-AFM, the inaugural KNILM flight from Batavia landed at Archerfield. Captain G. Van Messel and his aircraft stayed for only half an hour before continuing their journey to Sydney. An unprecedented five international flights passed through Brisbane that day as well as another twenty major interstate and local airline services.[28] But more important than the upsurge in aerial activity, this day witnessed a major step forward in linking Australia to the rest of the world by the latest and best aircraft.

Carrying the first outbound Empire air mail to Great Britain, *Camilla* is signalled to her buoy at Pinkenba by the DCA control launch on 4 August 1938. Gibson Island power station is in the background. (*Courier-Mail* photo via John Wilson)

For the next month the flying boats continued their "run-in" services. But on Thursday 4th August the service became fully operational when Captain Lester Brain lifted *Camilla* off Rose Bay with the first outbound mail under the Empire Air Mail scheme. The occasion was one of high publicity with *Camilla* being formally farewelled by Lord Huntingdale, acting Governor General of Australia.

Her departure was delayed for the ceremony and *Camilla* remained overnight at Pinkenba before resuming her journey at the scheduled time next morning.[29]

From now on, three flights a week would pass through Pinkenba in each direction carrying mail and passengers between Great Britain and Australia. The service was firmly established and flying boats to England became part of everyday life on the Brisbane River.

These flying boats benefited all Australians by the fast and relatively inexpensive delivery of mail to Great Britain. In their first season the Short Empires carried a record 244 tonnes of Christmas mail between England and Australia. By early September 1939 they had carried over 5,000 passengers and 500 tonnes of mail to Australia on the Empire air route.[30] The Empire air mail service brought a glamour to international flying boat travel which has never been surpassed. For the brief period these services operated, Short Empire flying boats represented the last word in comfort and sophistication in air travel.

Chapter 3 – The War Years

"Transport facilities are to be used for necessary purposes ... and fighting services get priority."[1]

The new international services continued for barely fourteen months before a shadow fell over their future. On 3 September 1939 war was declared between Great Britain, its Commonwealth and allies on the one hand and Germany on the other. The Second World War had commenced. Two Empire flying boats then in Sydney were requisitioned by the RAAF and the Empire air mail service reduced from three to two flights a week.

The early months of war did not go well for Great Britain and its allies. Italy took Germany's side on 10 June 1940 closing the Mediterranean to civil air traffic and cutting the Empire air link. A new route was devised which ran from Sydney to Durban via Cairo, bypassing the combat zone. Termed the "Horseshoe Route", it allowed mail and high priority passengers and cargo to reach Britain from Australia, carried on their final leg from Durban up the Atlantic by sea.

To meet wartime demands the flying boats were stripped of luxury passenger fittings and long range tanks were installed for extra endurance. Services commenced on 19 June 1940 to a twice weekly schedule. These continued with great success until the war reached the Pacific. During 1941 Qantas flying boats achieved their peak utilisation carrying 7,600 passengers, 264 tonnes of freight and 300 tonnes of mail between Sydney and Singapore.[2]

But Japan's rapid advance into Malaya, Singapore and the Dutch East Indies in December 1941 put Horseshoe Route aircraft at grave risk. The Short Empire *Corio* was shot down near Timor late in January 1942 and the link was finally broken on 14 February when Singapore surrendered.

Qantas flying boats were thrown into evacuating people in front of the Japanese advance and supporting military movements. An early operation carried out by *Centaurus* was delivering a contingent of American bomber and fighter pilots evacuated from the Philippines to Hamilton on Christmas Eve, 1941. Though the enemy advance then seemed unstoppable, these airmen became the nucleus for building an allied air force that would counter and overcome Japanese forces.[3]

The outbreak of war found the RAAF without any long range flying boats in Australia. Personnel of No. 10 Squadron were in England to collect nine fine new Sunderland maritime patrol flying boats. But they remained in Britain for the duration of the war, being joined by a second Sunderland squadron, No. 461, in 1942. Two Short Empires, *Centaurus* and *Calypso*, were impressed into RAAF service when war commenced, being joined by two more, *Coogee* and *Coolangatta*, in June the following year and a fifth, *Clifton*, in 1942. They were initially employed on maritime reconnaissance duties with No. 11 Squadron based at Port Moresby, but early in 1942 they became transports with a new unit, No. 33 Squadron.

The RAAF also ordered 18 Consolidated PBY-5 Catalina long range patrol flying boats from the USA. These were delivered across the Pacific by civilian Qantas crews as the USA was still neutral at this stage of the war. The first Catalina to make the crossing arrived in Australia on 2 February 1941. It was only the third aircraft to complete the trans-Pacific flight between America and Australia and the safe delivery of these aircraft in 1941 was a creditable achievement for Qantas. Catalinas became standard equipment for the RAAF with 168 being received during the war for four front line squadrons.

Short Empire *Coolangatta*, after joining the RAAF, rests in Hamilton Reach with the Meatworks beyond late in 1940. (photo courtesy Ian Beasley)

Qantas's flying boat base at Pinkenba had become well established since it opened in July 1938. But the terminal did not remain there for long. Brisbane's main sewerage pipeline collapsed at Pinkenba during April 1940 and temporary repairs directed untreated sewage into the river near the terminal. The stench became intolerable and on 16th Qantas moved its pontoon to a temporary location at the mouth of Breakfast Creek. A mooring buoy was laid in time for the incoming flight on the following day.[4]

Subsequently DCA built a landing stage, a small reception building and access roads just downstream from Hamilton Wharves. Mooring buoys remained at Pinkenba, but more were laid on the opposite side of the river at Colmslie. Hamilton Reach offered a landing and take off area 2½ kilometres long and it became the centre of Brisbane's flying boat operations for the rest of the war.

The Hamilton terminal and moorings were used by RAAF flying boats passing through Brisbane. In May 1942 a house at Langside Road, Hamilton Heights, was leased as a hostel for Catalina crews in Brisbane. It served this purpose as "Catalina House" for the remainder of the war. After the Coral Sea Battle Japanese submarines were active off eastern Australia and Catalinas patrolled from Brisbane for a short period on convoy protection duties.[5] But for most of the war maritime patrol in the Brisbane area was undertaken by land based Ansons and Beauforts.

As the war progressed Hamilton terminal became busier with the transit of both civil and military transport flying boats. The RAAF established its own base on the eastern side of the property with another jetty and service huts. This became RAAF Flying Boat Base, Hamilton which was controlled by No.5 Transport and Movements Office. Additional mooring buoys were laid with six each at Colmslie and Gibson Island.[6]

Qantas's hard-worked Short Empires suffered heavily on war service. Four were lost along with two of their RAAF sisters in the space of two months early in 1942, most to enemy action. All the RAAF's surviving Short Empires were returned in mid 1943, giving the airline three flying boats to operate a route from Sydney through Hamilton to Townsville for the Directorate of Civil Aviation. Two of these were lost in accidents later in the war. Six Sunderlands and a dozen Martin PBM-3R Mariner flying boats were delivered to the RAAF for transport purposes in 1944 equipping Nos. 40 and 41 Squadrons respectively. The Sunderlands operated largely between Townsville and New Guinea while the Mariners ranged more widely.

Hamilton became the southern terminus of No. 41 Squadron's route to Cairns on 4 July 1944, initially undertaking three flights a week, growing to a daily service as more aircraft came on line. On 15 August 1944 one of their Mariners proved the benefit of the long, continuous landing-ground represented by the Brisbane River. Just as it took off its port engine developed a fault, then burst into flames as a cylinder head blew out. Its pilot, Flight Lieutenant Roberts, shut down the engine and landed downwind at Pinkenba, about six kilometres from Hamilton. No one was hurt in the incident, but the aircraft's port engine and its mounting were destroyed.[7]

U.S. Navy seaplane base at Colmslie. (Official U.S. Navy photo, USNA: RG 71, *Defence-Aid Reciprocal Aid Review Board Report*, section 9 – item 52.)

Japan's entry into the war brought an influx of American forces into Australia. In July 1942 General Douglas MacArthur established headquarters for the Southwest Pacific theatre in Brisbane, and the numbers of American servicemen multiplied as the war progressed.

Demand quickly rose for transporting high priority passengers and official mail across the Pacific between the USA and Brisbane. Before the war Pan American Airways operated long distance flying boat services from America across the Pacific to the Philippines, China and New Zealand. Their expertise was recruited to organise flights to Brisbane for the United States Navy Air Transport Service (NATS). NATS quickly developed a seaplane base in Brisbane to receive these trans-Pacific flights and take care of air transport in the area.

A 16 hectare site was chosen at Colmslie on the opposite side of the river and a little further downstream from the Australian base at Hamilton. The property was resumed by the Australian Army and the U.S. Navy moved in on 9 September 1942.[8] The Americans immediately began clearing the site and

Queensland's Main Roads Commission was contracted to build a 12 metre wide stone slipway into the river for landing seaplanes. Completed by the beginning of December, the slipway was 76 metres long and extended to 2.4 metres below low water level. A paved hard standing area 61 metres square was built at the top of the slipway and access roadways were also constructed.[9] For the first time in Brisbane seaplanes could be beached for servicing ashore.

The base included a 30 metres square workshop and administration building, a slightly smaller store (27 x 15 metres) and a complete aviation gasoline fuelling system. Barracks on a rise behind the parking area could accommodate 120 officers and enlisted men, including up to 92 transient personnel. Other facilities on site included a weather station, vehicle pool and launches using a 66 metre jetty specially rebuilt for the base. Total cost was US$124,536.37, mostly in reverse lend lease funds.[10] The new base was more comprehensive than any seaplane facilities previously seen on the Brisbane River.

Occupying the same site was the U.S. Navy's Radio Brisbane. This was an important strategic installation communicating from Seventh Fleet headquarters in Brisbane to units throughout the Southwest Pacific as well as to Pearl Harbor and Washington.

The U.S. Naval Seaplane Base was primarily a transport centre and its staffing reflected civil involvement. Out of the base's 16 administration personnel, twelve were responsible for NATS operations while eight of these, including six officers, managed the Pan Am activities of NATS. While their aircraft carried military markings, the flying boat service was widely recognised as being provided by the airline. The transport flying boats used by the Americans to fly to Brisbane were mainly twin engine Martin PBM-3 Mariners possessing a long range and lifting a payload of 4,086 kg or 20 passengers. Larger four engine Consolidated Coronado flying boats were also used, their reverse pitch propellers greatly improving their manoeuvrability on the water. An average of ten transient aircraft a week passed through the base with a passenger capacity of 250 and cargo capacity of 34,050 kg.[11]

Commander Arthur McCollum flew into Brisbane's seaplane base soon after it was opened in 1942. In Pearl Harbor he was told "If you're going to Australia, you've got to go to Brisbane anyway, because you go by plane and that's the only way the planes fly." It was a "hairy" trip. "These planes were operated under contract by the Pan American Airways … and they were Martin flying boats. … These planes were not soundproofed, … and they were pretty damned noisy. You couldn't even talk to people in them. Didn't have all these cute stewardesses running around like they have nowadays." After having to turn back three times his aircraft finally completed the first leg of the journey to

Canton Island. There it was delayed for an engine change while McCollum waited three days in the Pan Am Hotel before continuing on to Suva, Noumea, and finally Brisbane.[12]

Four U.S. Navy flying boats moored off Colmslie in March 1944. (Official U.S. Navy photo, USNA, RG 80-G, 230050)

In addition to the trans-Pacific trunk route from Brisbane through Noumea, NATS flying boats flew regularly south to Sydney and north to Townsville where they connected with other flights to ports throughout the Southwest Pacific.

As well as providing a terminus for trans-Pacific transports, in mid 1943 Brisbane also became a rallying point for American patrol flying boats. The U.S. Seventh Fleet was formed in Brisbane on 15 March 1943, leading to a build up of forces in the Southwest Pacific for offensive operations against the Japanese. On 27th June Captain T.S. Coombs took command of the Seventh Fleet's air arm and immediately brought VP-101, a long range patrol squadron equipped with Catalinas, from Perth to Brisbane for operations in New Guinea. An advance flight left for Port Moresby on 1 July, being followed by further aircraft later in the month. Forward support equipment and personnel belonging to VP-101 sailed from Brisbane in the seaplane tender USS *San Pablo* during July to set up base in the Milne Bay area. Two months later a second Catalina squadron arrived, VP-11, enabling the U.S. Navy's Patrol Wing 17 to be commissioned in Brisbane on 15 September 1943.[13]

The U.S. Navy Catalinas, together with those of the RAAF's front line squadrons, were fitted with radar enabling them to patrol enemy waters at night to intercept Japanese shipping. They also conducted night raids on enemy bases. Because of their predominantly night operations and very dark camouflage painting, they quickly became known as "Black Cats". The "Black Cats" of both nations would go on to write their own heroic chapter in the story of World War Two.

After the American invasion of the Philippines in October 1944, Southwest Pacific headquarters moved north and military activity around Brisbane diminished. Faster land planes were also becoming available for NATS to use on the Brisbane-Noumea route. By December 1944 land based DC3 and Liberator transports had completely taken over the service, and the U.S. Seaplane Base at Colmslie was decommissioned on the 6th.[14] The seaplane base was handed back to the Australian Government on 9 January 1945 whilst the remainder of the property with Radio Brisbane was returned on 27 March.[15]

General Douglas MacArthur (centre) greets Vice Admiral Halsey (left) arriving by flying boat at Colmslie in 1943. (Official U.S. Navy photo, USNA, RG 80-G, 394405)

At this time the British Pacific Fleet was being built up in Australia for operations against Japan and the seaplane base was taken over by the Royal Navy. However, the British fleet had only one squadron of seaplanes and these moved to Hong Kong before the end of the year, leaving the Colmslie base empty.

At the end of the war the RAAF had a strong force of Catalina flying boats as well as its Mariner and Sunderland transports. They were immediately redirected to repatriation duties across the Southwest Pacific with priority being given to carrying prisoners of war home to Australia. They continued with these activities for most of the next year, then most were mothballed or put up for sale. By April 1946 the RAAF base at Hamilton was no longer needed and its jetty dismantled and buildings sold.[16] Only a handful of Catalinas remained in service for peacetime search and rescue duties.

Chapter 4 – Return to Peace

The end of the war had been scented; the old dark days were passing, … and England, the USA, and the other Allies and neutrals were setting their eyes on the expected great era of long range air transport which now so obviously lay ahead.[1]

While repatriation and demobilisation were restoring lives disrupted by war, airlines began reconstructing their businesses for peace. Throughout the Pacific war Qantas was absorbed in transport for the war effort. Its splendid fleet of Short Empire flying boats that were the last word in aviation when hostilities began, had been decimated. Only one survived to see the peace, *Coriolanus.* Originally belonging to Imperial Airways, she was east of Singapore when the Japanese struck and transferred to Qantas as VH-ABG.

Coriolanus about to touch down at Hamilton in March 1947 with Bulimba Hill in the background. (*Courier-Mail* photo via John Wilson)

With *Coriolanus*, Qantas began the readjustment to peace, using her to fly the first post-war charter to Singapore on 4 October 1945. Six weeks later, on 19 November, she opened services on an unscheduled basis from Sydney to Suva.[2] These flights took two days in each direction, passing through Brisbane with an overnight stop-over in Noumea.[3] *Coriolanus* continued running these flights for two years. But after logging a total of 4,061,295 kilometres, she was withdrawn from service, arriving in Sydney from her final flight on 20 December 1947.[4] Qantas was then left only with Catalina flying boats.

Meanwhile civil air services to England reopened. An express air mail service using Avro Lancastrians, converted Lancaster bombers, carrying a handful of passengers in austere conditions was introduced as the war ended. Introducing a more comfortable peacetime passenger service between England and Australia was an urgent priority.

Taking up where the pre-war Short Empires left off, Great Britain converted some Short Sunderlands to carry passengers on what was now called the "Kangaroo Route". All the Sunderlands belonged to BOAC, which had succeeded Imperial Airways in 1940, and were known as their "Hythe" class.

The first service departed Sydney on Sunday 19 May 1946 with Qantas crews flying the Singapore to Sydney sector of the route. Peacetime standards had returned with the Hythes providing luxury travel for 16 passengers including sleeping berths, in-flight cabin service and a spacious promenade area. The flying boats departed from Rose Bay, Sydney, on three nights per week, overflying Brisbane to their first stop at Bowen. Hamilton was kept open as an alternative set down area with staff being advised from Rose Bay if a landing was required.[5]

The Hythes were no faster than the Short Empires from which they were developed and their passenger capacity was no greater. Their longer range reduced refuelling stops and flying day and night their initial schedule cut their predecessor's time to England almost in half to 5½ days.[6] But this proved impractical and uneconomical. After six months their timetable was stretched out by a further two days with just one overnight flight scheduled in each direction.[7]

As it was before the war, comfort was featured and flying to England only remained possible for those with deep pockets. A single fare between England and Australia was £325, equivalent to a year's wages or half the cost of a house for an average working man.[8] In the event, senior government officials and business executives filled most of the Hythes' passenger lists.[9]

However, attitudes had changed since the war. Fast, long distance flying had become commonplace and, taking more than double the time of the competing Lancastrians, the flying boats were only a temporary solution. When the Hythe service began the press reported it with only a brief paragraph – a far cry from the extensive coverage that accompanied each pre-war initiative.[10] In addition, Australia no longer felt compelled to buy British when far better airliners were available from the USA. Without any aircraft of their own flying the Kangaroo Route, Qantas purchased a fleet of Lockheed Constellation long-range airliners which combined the Lancastrian's speed with the Hythe's comfort.

BOAC Hythe flying boat *Howard* at Hamilton in April 1946 after being diverted due to bad weather between Bowen and Sydney. These aircraft began regular services to England in the following month. (*Courier-Mail* photo via John Wilson)

Qantas Constellations commenced operating to Britain in December 1947 in parallel with the Hythes. The flying boats' timetable was further revised, shaving off half a day in each direction, but at the cost of a second overnight flight.[11] This, coupled with early starts on other days and a week of long hours in the air, tested the passengers' stamina. But the unequal competition could not last and BOAC also obtained Constellations to replace their older flying boats. The last Hythe, *Honduras*, left Rose Bay for England on 6 February 1949. In over two and a half years on the Kangaroo Route, the BOAC Hythes covered 16 million kilometres, carrying 31,000 passengers.[12]

****

As soon as the war ended the DCA terminal at Hamilton was upgraded to handle civilian flights and passengers.[13] Located on Crown land at the downstream end of Hamilton Wharves, the terminal included a complex of buildings with a 12.2 x 9.1 metres passenger reception area, a workshop, floating pontoon, access roads and car parking. Three mooring buoys were maintained off the southern riverbank with passengers being ferried to their aircraft by launch.[14] The distance was not far as the river here was barely half a kilometre wide.

Brisbane's flying boat terminal at Hamilton in August 1951. (NAA Brisbane: BP292/1, 214/108/1 Part 2, attached to DoI Property Survey Branch memo, 24 August 1951)

Take offs and landings took place on the eastern half of Hamilton Reach downstream from the Apollo Ferry. Here the river stretches straight ahead for two kilometres before turning gently into Quarries Reach. The area suited most weather conditions for Brisbane, but when a strong south-westerly cross-wind was blowing flying boats were forced to operate from Pinkenba or the Quarries Reach.

Control over Brisbane's air space was exercised from the control tower at Eagle Farm airport. However actual flying boat movements at Hamilton were supervised by the DCA Control Officer at the flying boat base. The Department's launches performed a vital role sweeping the area to keep it free of obstructions, laying a flare path of lighted buoys if needed after dark, advising tide and wind, and standing by during the take off or landing.[15]

Commercial launches were engaged in ferrying passengers, refuelling and servicing flying boats at their moorings.

Not all agreed that Hamilton was suitable for the resumption of peacetime flying boat services through Brisbane. Before the war Pinkenba had been preferred because Hamilton Reach was considered too congested for flying boats to operate with safety. But the war years saw the water airport move to Hamilton anyway, and a new seaplane base with beaching facilities was built across the river at Colmslie. Under emergency war programmes new wharves and Cairncross graving dock were built in Hamilton Reach, increasing shipping movements on this confined stretch of water. The risk of an accident had multiplied and this concerned Brisbane's port authorities.

Even before the war ended they campaigned to move flying boats away from Hamilton. Three days after victory had been won in Europe the Queensland Premier wrote to the Prime Minister asking that flying boat operations be moved from Hamilton back to Pinkenba. This was answered, not surprisingly, by pointing out that extensive facilities had been built at Colmslie, and it was not appropriate to make any change as the Pacific war was not yet over.[16]

Immediately after Japan was defeated the Premier raised the issue once again. The Prime Minister replied that flying boats were currently using Hamilton Reach to repatriate service personnel including former prisoners of war.[17] Brisbane's port authorities never wavered from their view that flying boats at Hamilton constituted an unacceptable risk, causing the Queensland Premier to write repeatedly to the Prime Minister urging that the moorings at Hamilton be removed.[18]

The Civil Aviation Department sought a solution, commencing negotiations with ACF Shirleys in December 1946 to lease part of their property at Pinkenba for use by flying boats. But these discussions ended when it was learned a planned railway extension would cut across any slipway or hard standing area on the site.[19]

From the Portmaster's viewpoint the problem of flying boats at Hamilton escalated each year. Shipping movements on the Brisbane River rose steadily from 597 in 1947 to 838 in 1950.[20] In addition, new berths E and F (now Maritime Wharves) built for overseas shipping in 1950 would see large vessels swinging directly opposite the flying boat buoys at Colmslie.[21] His concerns were fortified by complaints from ship-owners when flying boats delayed the movement of their ships. The Portmaster would not be satisfied until flying boat operations moved downstream below Pinkenba Wharf.[22]

The problem with Hamilton – the 11,000 ton *Suffolk* fills the Brisbane River as she passes the flying boat base landing stage and crash launches. (photo courtesy Frank Kelly)

But the Portmaster had some opposition. The chief flying boat operator out of Brisbane at this time was Barrier Reef Airways, which enjoyed the Queensland Premier's support for their tourist operations to the north.[23] The airline opposed the Portmaster's attempt to have seaplanes move from Hamilton to Pinkenba as the extra distance would be a considerable inconvenience in handling its passengers.[24] Barrier Reef's owner and manager, Stewart Middlemiss, vigorously pressed his airline's interests with both State and Federal Governments, and closely followed every development in the search for a better location for Brisbane's water airport.

Meanwhile the Department of Civil Aviation was investigating other possible sites on the Brisbane River. Plans were drawn up to acquire a former Navy oil depot at the mouth of Aquarium Passage at Hemmant in 1949. But these were abandoned as the local authority required the property for a roadway.[25] Other sites at Doboy Creek, Gibson Island and Lytton Quarantine Station were considered but these were either too remote or undeveloped.

A breakthrough came in December 1950. On the 12th the Regional Director of Civil Aviation in Brisbane received a telegram from his Director General for "immediate purchase blocks at Pinkenba. Register our claim immediately….

Letter on above lines being forwarded to Premier through PM Department. Essential we obtain approval from above."[26]

The State Government was prepared to offer a 15 year lease for a flying boat base on land at the outermost limit of development at Pinkenba. The opportunity was not to be missed. Plans were drawn up for a five hectare site adjoining Shell Oil Company's property. These included a slipway, hard stand and hangar, as well as an embarkation pontoon. Alighting areas 2.3 kilometres long were available on either side of the proposed base in upper and lower Lytton Reach which could be used day or night.[27] The only condition remaining was that the plans were acceptable to Brisbane's harbour authorities.

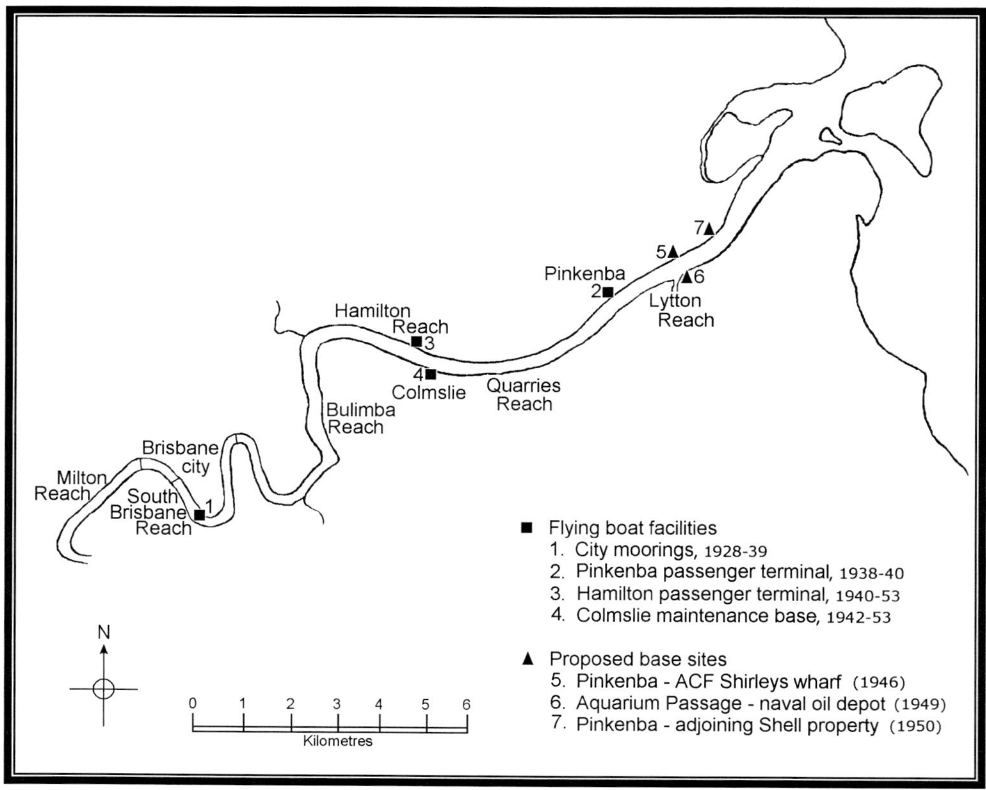

Map 2 – Brisbane River flying boat sites

Chapter 5 – Barrier Reef Airways

"Fly, and just a few hours from Brisbane you'll touch down on the smooth water of a tropic lagoon – to relax and laze away the sunny days of your precious vacation."[1]

Following demobilisation at the end of the war, Catalina pilot Stewart Middlemiss was keen to remain in aviation, seeing a vision of flying tourists into Great Barrier Reef resort islands by flying boat. In 1946 he approached Chris Poulson, proprietor of Heron Island, who saw how flying his guests in would save them from a rough boat trip and a partnership was formed trading as Barrier Reef Airways. There was an added attraction of flying into nearby Gladstone which did not have a regular airline service at that time. With limited capital of £1,000 they bought three relatively new Catalinas from the RAAF that October.

The ex-USN seaplane base at Colmslie was ideally situated as a base for the proposed airline. It was across the river from Brisbane's flying boat terminal and aircraft could be beached for servicing ashore. Agreement was reached with the Navy to use the site and Middlemiss and his small team of ex-servicemen moved in and started work. The first of the airline's Catalinas, VH-BRA named *The Beachcomber*, completed its conversion around the middle of 1947. From its home on the Brisbane River, Queensland's own flying boat airline would soon be making regular flights to Heron Island, Gladstone and the Whitsunday Islands.[2]

Barrier Reef Airways was launched in style with an official opening by the Lieutenant Governor, Hon F.G. Cooper, on 2 July 1947. Guests included Deputy Premier Vince Gair, reflecting support the airline enjoyed from the Queensland Government. In his opening speech Mr Cooper highlighted the unique contribution the airline would make to Queensland.

> "Such an air service can attract holiday makers from southern States – people with only a short time to enjoy a holiday, and who would not come here if they had to spend much of their leave travelling by train or boat. Now it will be possible to travel all the way by air from the cold of the South to Queensland's sun-shine centres."[3]

At the conclusion of formalities guests were taken on a one hour flight over Brisbane. Operations commenced ten days later when Middlemiss lifted *Beachcomber* off Hamilton Reach bound for Gladstone and Heron Island. The first service into the Whitsundays took place on 21st July to Lindeman and Daydream islands.

Their inaugural schedule provided flights from Brisbane to Heron Island and Gladstone each Friday and Saturday, and to the Whitsunday Islands each Monday, landing at Lindeman and either Daydream or South Molle. Most flights departed Brisbane at 6am, but during the winter months the round trip to the Whitsundays, 960km from Brisbane, could not be completed in daylight. On these occasions departure was delayed to 10am with the flying boat staying overnight at Daydream, completing the return journey next morning.[4]

Flight times offered spectacular savings over alternative transport. The 560km flight to Heron Island took 2 hours 20 minutes compared with 15 hours on board a train from Brisbane to Gladstone followed by a six or seven hour boat trip to the island. Time savings to the Whitsundays were even more dramatic. Travel from Brisbane by train, bus and launch took over two days whereas a Catalina flew there in four hours.[5]

Barrier Reef Airways' first aircraft, the Catalina *Beachcomber*, is towed to her moorings during 1949 with the airline's maintenance base at Colmslie behind.
(NAA image A1200, L11841 via John Wilson)

Passengers arrived at the Queensland Government Tourist Bureau office an hour before departure time and were taken to the Hamilton terminal for their luggage to be loaded. From there they travelled to the flying boat aboard a launch operated by Norman Wright under contract with the airline. Frank Kelly, one of Barrier Reef's inaugural pilots, describes what this was like.

"If we had a high tide at Heron at 6 in the morning we could operate two hours either side... Our passengers originally had to wait at Adelaide Street outside the Tourist Bureau. They were our agents [and] they did not open till the morning. So they're standing out there on a cold windy morning waiting for a bus to come... People were used to that sort of air travel in those days."[6]

Once aboard, passengers found the Catalina had been refurbished to airliner standard. Adjustable, upholstered seats were provided in three compartments for 22 passengers and its interior had been lined for greater comfort. A meal was served in flight, but as the Catalinas had no cooking facilities on board, they were cold meals billed as "tropical salads", prepared before departure by Kelly's wife.[7] The fledgling airline got away to a good start. Around 1,000 passenger were carried in its first two months with arriving and departing guests providing good passenger loadings in each direction.[8]

The airline suffered an early setback when, on 28 November 1947, Chris Poulson was lost at sea. *Beachcomber* carried out an aerial search but all that was found was Poulson's upturned dinghy some miles away. Middlemiss paid out the Poulson estate's share in the airline with some difficulty but continued the business. His wife Hope helped as the airline's hostess on charter flights, and he acted as traffic clerk, bus driver, chief engineer and pilot.[9]

****

The heat and rain of summer brought a reduction in tourist activity in the tropics and some of the resorts closed down altogether. After Christmas, flights to the Whitsundays were suspended until the end of March and those to Heron Island were reduced to one a week, ceasing for six weeks at the end of January 1948.[10]

After the airline's first year its schedule stabilised to three flights a week, one to Heron Island on Saturday and two to the Whitsundays on Tuesday and Sunday.[11] The steeply shelving beach allowed flying boats to anchor close to shore at Daydream Island, and this became established as the flying boat's main arrival point in the northern Whitsundays. Passengers for South Molle and Long Island resorts were carried the short distance to their destination by launch.[12] "Catalina Days" were special at Daydream. Lunch was served in two sittings to cater for the extra visitors and bar takings were highest.[13]

With limited staff numbers and building up his market, Middlemiss looked for ways of minimising his airline's costs and increasing its income. He challenged the imposition of Federal Government air route charges, claiming they were inappropriate for flying boat landing areas – but without success.[14] Also, with one Catalina in service, progress on converting his second aircraft to carry passengers was slow due to the cash outlays involved.

Barrier Reef Airways inaugural flying boat captains, Stewart Middlemiss (left), owner, manager and pilot, and Frank Kelly (right), assistant manager and pilot.
(photo courtesy Frank Kelly)

The airline also sought new business opportunities in special charters and new ports to service. In December 1947 *Beachcomber* flew a special charter to Merauke in West New Guinea to transfer a tug crew. A special Christmas flight was run to Sydney in 1947 as well as additional Christmas and New Year services to Heron Island and Gladstone.[15] The airline's profile was also enhanced by media opportunities. These included reporting the progress of yachts off Fraser Island in the 1950 Brisbane to Gladstone ocean yacht race for a local radio station, and giving joy flights from Cleveland for Redlands' centenary in December that year.[16]

But of more permanent benefit was extending the airline's route network to new destinations and broadening its client base. Plans to include Dunk Island, Urangan and Ballina to the airline's schedule did not proceed. Although granted a licence to fly into Grafton in February 1950, post-war rationing of aviation fuel prevented the airline from commencing services there at that time.[17] But adding Hayman Island to their Whitsundays network in 1950 proved highly successful.

As a young man before the war, Middlemiss had learned to fly in a school run by Reginald Ansett and they knew each other well. Late in June 1947, as Barrier Reef Airways' first commercial engagement, Ansett chartered *Beachcomber* for a four day tour visiting seven towns and islands along the Queensland coast.[18] During this tour he visited Hayman Island and leased it for development as a tourist resort.

The high class resort took three years to build and was more luxurious than anything else in the tropics. Following the resort's opening in July 1950 Barrier Reef Airways included Hayman in its Whitsunday itinerary, adding an extra flight there from Brisbane each Friday.[19] By 1954 over 70% of Hayman guests were travelling in by flying boat.[20]

While the airline consolidated its market profile, a shadow hung over its maintenance base at Colmslie. From the outset Barrier Reef Airways was competing for space with the Army which had taken over the property for use by its water transport arm. The Army fenced off the buildings already on the site, allowing the airline only the beaching ramp and the small hard standing area. In the river, Army vessels and moorings crowded around the ramp, cramping flying boat movements.[21]

Even before the airline had begun operations Middlemiss complained "we are now unable to establish ourselves with any degree of permanency" and urged the DCA to find a more permanent base on the river.[22] The Army did ask for the flying boat base to be returned in March 1951, but nothing came of these plans and Barrier Reef Airways was still on the property two years later.

Colmslie was less than satisfactory in other respects. Consisting only of an open area with an aging slipway, the airline erected two small workshop buildings but there was no hangar for its aircraft. After three years of successful operations Middlemiss complained to the Director General of Civil Aviation of the "backyard conditions" in which he was still forced to maintain and service his airline's growing fleet.[23]

The slipway was in a poor state of repair. Built on a stone foundation its surface of wartime "Marsden Matting" had rusted and needed resurfacing. By November 1949 the broken ramp had already caused six punctured tyres and urgent repairs were needed before more serious damage occurred.[24] Ever mindful of these concerns, Middlemiss persistently lobbied for a permanent flying boat base to be established on the river and took a close interest in all DCA's steps in seeking a new site.

"Backyard conditions" at Colmslie – Barrier Reef Airways flying boats parked at Colmslie in August 1951. (NAA Brisbane: BP292/1, 214/108/1 Part 2, attached to DoI Property Survey Branch memo, 24 August 1951)

****

Middlemiss purchased three relatively new Catalinas in 1946 and another five next year, most of which were used for spare parts. Two were registered in 1947 as VH-BRA and VH-BRB. But priority was given to completing VH-

BRA, *Beachcomber*, to ensure the airline's services commenced as quickly as possible. Due to cash limitations, work on fitting out VH-BRB for service was slow and operations continued with just a single aircraft.

Nevertheless perceptions were important and Middlemiss encouraged the belief that his fleet was stronger than it was. Two Catalinas were already registered and his publicity brochure stated "Flagship and first aircraft in service with Barrier Reef Airways is the *Beachcomber*. Sister ships are the *Buccaneer* and the *Bermuda*."[25] Nevertheless, for the airline's first two years *Beachcomber* operated alone, faithfully maintaining the airline's schedule and establishing the fragile business on a firm footing. Frank Kelly recalls:

> "We didn't miss a service with this aircraft. We only had one aircraft. We had this fleet of aircraft over at Colmslie. None of them would fly... We flew with one aircraft all that time and we didn't miss a service."[26]

Catalina *Beachcomber* at Daydream Island. (Mervyn Jones)

Barrier Reef's second Catalina, VH-BRB *Buccaneer*, completed fitting out and passed its certification trials on 18 March 1949.[27] *Buccaneer* took over the workload while *Beachcomber* came ashore for an overhaul and rest. The third Catalina, *Bermuda*, never entered service with the airline and was sold.

The airline's first mishap occurred on 31 January 1950 when *Buccaneer* was put out of action in an accident at Daydream Island. An engine failed to start for take off and the aircraft drifted into a nearby launch damaging the wing and an engine.[28] The disabled Catalina was towed to Bowen where she was beached and repaired. As these events occurred during the slack summer season, services were not disrupted.

At the time of this incident Barrier Reef Airways was considering an opportunity to greatly improve its fleet. Late in 1949 TEAL offered four Short Sandringhams for sale, but the price of £5,000 each was a serious obstacle for Barrier Reef Airways. Nevertheless, these aircraft were a significant advance on the airline's Catalinas. They offered passengers greater comfort, safety, and speed, as well as hot meals served from a large buffet area. Ansett came to Barrier Reef's help, financing the purchase of two Sandringhams by buying a 51% share in the airline.[29] With this controlling interest Barrier Reef Airways was added to Ansett's growing business empire.

The two Sandringhams arrived in Brisbane during April 1950 with the first, VH-BRC entering service the following month. Initially named *Coral Clipper*, this was soon abandoned as Pan Am held exclusive rights to the name "Clipper".[30] The second Sandringham, VH-BRD required some modifications and did not enter service until April 1951.[31]

At the time the new Sandringhams arrived, Hayman Island resort was nearing completion and VH-BRC was used to fly in materials to finish the resort's fitting out. Then the airline ferried 80 guests in for the official opening on 3 July 1950.[32] These included the Deputy Prime Minister and Treasurer, Hon Arthur Fadden, three other Federal Ministers and the State Minister for Transport. It was a chance to show off the new Sandringhams to these influential guests and Middlemiss noted all "expressed their satisfaction of our services."[33]

The arrival of the four engine, double-deck Sandringhams lifted spirits at the airline. But their acquisition stretched Barrier Reef Airways' facilities to the limit. The added pressure of handling thirty passengers per flight was resolved when the airline took over full use of the Hamilton passenger terminal. But the heavier Sandringhams needed the slipway and parking area at Colmslie strengthened. Submissions were made to the Commonwealth to have the ramp resurfaced in concrete and lengthened after a Sandringham had become bogged. The airline also asked for an extension to its hard-standing area, but in the end nothing was done.[34]

The Sandringhams were too large to land and take off in Heron Island's lagoon so Catalinas continued services there once or twice a week. The new Sandringhams added luxury to the Whitsunday services, running three times a week during the high season to Lindeman, Daydream and Hayman Islands.[35] The Sandringhams' schedule was extended to Townsville in June 1951 as a first step in building a tour route from Hayman Island. Pilots disliked landing at Townsville as the aircraft alighted in the sea outside the harbour, then taxied between the arms of the breakwater and all the way up harbour to moor. Sandringhams were also made available for charter and in this way made several trips to Hobart for Trans Oceanic Airways.[36]

Barrier Reef Airways Sandringham VH-BRD (*Princess of Cairns*) at her moorings off Colmslie in 1951. (Mervyn Jones)

As a result of Ansett's financing their Sandringham purchase, Barrier Reef Airways became part of the Ansett Transport Industries group. The airline continued to trade under its own name but bookings were handled by Ansett Airways and passengers checked in at the Ansett office at 95 North Quay, Brisbane. Ansett gave Barrier Reef Airways strength and stability it had never enjoyed before, and with its expanded fleet, the airline extended its route network over the next two years.

Approval was given to fly into Sydney in January 1951, but it was not until 1 July 1951 that *Buccaneer* inaugurated this service.[37] A series of special flights were added over the Christmas and New Year period of 1951-52 as well as for the following Easter.[38] In June 1952 Grafton was added as an intermediate stop on the Sydney route which was flown initially on a Friday but quickly escalated to a Monday also.[39]

In the following month Southport became a port of call on the Sydney service. Trans Oceanic Airways initially gained approval to operate into Southport's

Broadwater in June 1952 with local businessman Bernard Elsey as their local agent. But when this airline went into liquidation less than a month later, arrangements to use the Broadwater as well as Elsey's services, were quickly taken over by Ansett. Flying boat facilities on the Southport Broadwater were basic with a mooring buoy just north-east of the entrance to Biggera Creek and a 2,750 metre alighting area stretching away at 010° northwards past where Runaway Bay now stands.[40]

The first service from Brisbane to Sydney via Southport and Grafton was flown on 25 July 1952. Flying boats landing on the Southport Broadwater proved so popular that Ansett financed the sealing of Coolangatta aerodrome so his own airliners could fly in on a more frequent basis.[41] After less than two years, in March 1954, Ansett ceased running flying boats through Southport and in the following October the mooring buoy was removed and Southport's water airport closed.[42]

The tourist route from Hayman was extended to Cairns with services commencing on 31 May 1952 and continuing through the high season winter months. Flights left Brisbane at 8.30am each Thursday and Saturday with the aircraft making one stop in the Whitsundays on its way to Townsville and then Cairns where it was scheduled to arrive at 4pm. The aircraft stayed overnight in Cairns before retracing its steps to Brisbane next day.[43]

But parallel with these route expansions came a corporate change making Ansett's take-over of Barrier Reef Airways complete. Ansett bought out Stewart Middlemiss's remaining share holding in Barrier Reef Airways and on 1 May 1952 the airline became Ansett Flying Boat Services Pty Ltd. The name Barrier Reef Airways lingered as its trading banner for a few months, but from 31 March 1953 both aircraft and operations were fully identified as Ansett Flying Boat Services.[44]

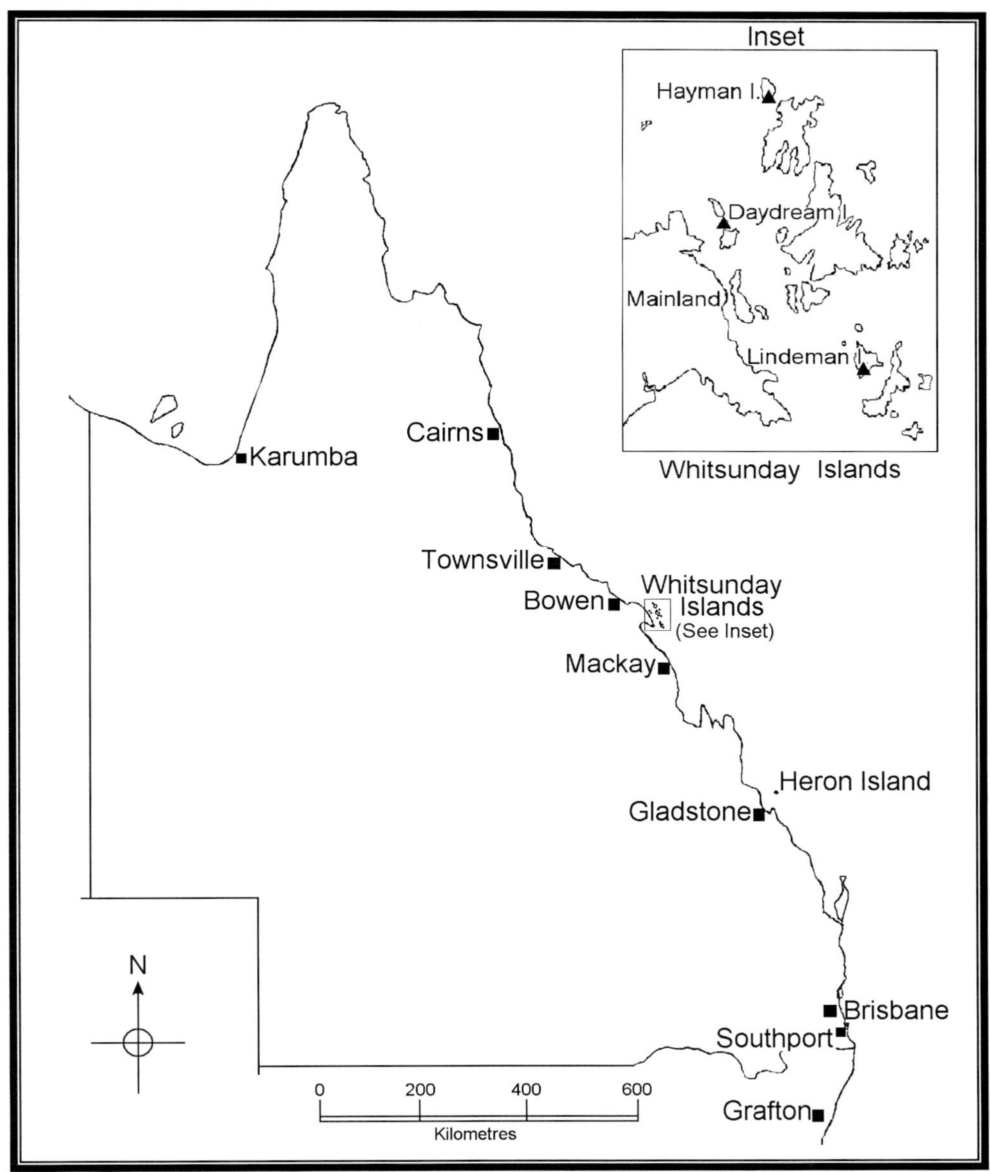

Map 3 – Flying boat destinations in Queensland

Chapter 6 – Widening Horizons

"If my aeroplane could fly three hundred miles it must be possible some day to fly three thousand miles to join the continents across the oceans. If people could be brought together... they would learn to know each other:"[1]

By the early 1950s, peacetime airline services had become fully established after the war and Australian flying boats widened their horizons to new and more exotic destinations. During this time the Brisbane River witnessed the last great pioneering trans-oceanic flight by a flying boat.

P.G. Taylor aboard *Frigate Bird II.* (Australian War Memorial, negative no. P02948.003)

On the evening of 20 April 1951, Captain P.G. Taylor brought his Catalina *Frigate Bird II* to rest at Hamilton having crossed the South Pacific Ocean from Australia to South America and back. These were the first flights between these continents on either side of the Pacific, and they crowned a glittering career of pioneer ocean navigation and flying. Taylor had accompanied Sir Charles Kingsford Smith on the first eastbound Pacific crossing in 1934, and in the following year gained heroic fame by saving the *Southern Cross* when it was crippled far out over the Tasman Sea. He captained the first flight across the Indian Ocean from Australia to Africa in 1939 and pioneered a South Pacific air route from Mexico to Australia in 1944.

Seeing air services between Australia and South America as the last world air link still to be established, he obtained *Frigate Bird II* from the RAAF, and departed Sydney on 13 March 1951. *Frigate Bird II* arrived in Valparaiso two weeks later via Fiji, Samoa, Tonga, Tahiti, Mangareve and Easter Island. After staying a week in Chile, Taylor and his crew returned by the same route, planning to arrive in Sydney on 21 April after a journey of 27,000 kilometres.

His last overnight stop was intended to be Lord Howe Island, but an adverse weather report forced a diversion elsewhere. With a reception planned for his arrival in Sydney, Taylor chose Brisbane. *Frigate Bird II* touched down at 6.25pm before continuing to Sydney next morning.[2] The flight was a magnificent achievement which Qantas founder Hudson Fysh described "as one of the greatest pioneering flights in the world's history of aviation."[3]

But Taylor had other news which grabbed the headlines in Brisbane. Stepping off the aircraft with Taylor was an attractive young lady in air hostess uniform, Miss Joyce Kennington. She and Taylor had just become engaged to be married and she had joined the homeward flight in Tahiti.[4] Gordon Taylor was subsequently knighted for his aviation achievements and *Frigate Bird II* is now displayed with honour in Sydney's Powerhouse Museum.

A month after Taylor's return, on 26 May 1951 another survey flight took off from Hamilton. But this was a very different mission with a practical objective. Instead of setting out into the Pacific, this aircraft turned west for the Indian Ocean. The aircraft was a Qantas Catalina piloted by Captain L.J. Grey carrying a party of twelve aviation specialists to remote Cocos Island. The team included experts from Qantas, DCA, RAAF and RAN who would investigate the work needed to make Cocos Island suitable as a staging point for intercontinental air services. The Catalina was loaded with all the bedding, food and fuel needed to make the party self-sufficient for their stay on the island. Three weeks later they returned to Brisbane with their survey successfully completed.[5]

As a result of their work an international airport and support facilities was built on Cocos Island making a direct air link between Australia and South Africa feasible. Seven months later a Qantas Constellation landed on the new Cocos Island airstrip during a proving flight from Perth to Johannesburg. Regular services commenced on 1 September 1952.

While Qantas was using a new generation of land based airliners to expand its international routes, the airline had improved its flying boat fleet with modern peacetime aircraft. Qantas had purchased several surplus Catalinas from the RAAF which were used for services from Sydney to Lord Howe Island, Fiji and the New Hebrides. In 1950 Qantas bought two Sandringhams from TEAL. The Sandringhams were introduced on the South Pacific run in June 1950, but a year later one was written off in an accident at Vila. Qantas bought three more from BOAC, the last being delivered in December 1951.[6]

Now with a fleet of four Sandringhams and four Catalinas, Qantas expanded its flying boat routes. The Catalinas were based at Port Moresby to service the network of coastal settlements and islands around New Guinea, while the Sandringhams operated out of Sydney on the long haul to Noumea, Fiji and the New Hebrides.[7]

Qantas Catalina *Island Chieftain* at Samarai, Papua New Guinea in 1957.
(Mervyn Jones)

Since the end of the war Qantas had relied on land planes to link eastern Australian cities with New Guinea. The DC3s that originally ran from Sydney via ports to Port Moresby and Lae were supplemented by four engine DC4 Skymasters on the "Bird of Paradise" route in March 1950. Two years later Qantas Sandringhams also began operating to Port Moresby.

These enhanced operations brought Qantas flying boats again onto the Brisbane River on a scheduled basis. The first change occurred in the Sandringhams' service from Sydney to Noumea which had previously flown direct from Sydney, bypassing Brisbane. From 17 June 1952 Brisbane was included in the outward leg of this service with flying boats calling on Tuesdays bound for the New Hebrides, and Thursdays for Suva. Arriving from Sydney at 6.30am, passengers were brought ashore and bussed to Eagle Farm airport for breakfast, resuming their journey two hours later.[8] But with a 3.15am departure from Rose Bay this was not a convenient arrangement. It was discontinued after two months as Sandringhams returned to a dawn departure from Sydney, flying to Noumea direct.[9]

Qantas Sandringhams began operating the Sydney-Port Moresby service in July 1952 with Brisbane included as an intermediate stop in both directions. The route was serviced fortnightly with Sandringhams passing through Hamilton northbound every second Saturday morning, returning late on the Friday afternoon two weeks later. During its twelve days in New Guinea, the flying boat worked a busy programme servicing up to 17 towns and communities from the Fly River District in the west to Samarai, Rabaul and Bougainville in the east.[10]

Like Stewart Middlemiss who translated his wartime flying boat experience into Barrier Reef Airways, another wartime flying boat pilot, Bryan Monkton had a similar vision of creating a flying boat airline to operate out of Sydney. His airline, Trans Oceanic Airways Pty Ltd, was incorporated on 24 February 1947 to run charters and regular services to Lord Howe Island and Grafton. Monkton bought a fleet of surplus Sunderlands from the RAAF which were fitted out initially with passenger seats and, like their BOAC contemporaries, were called Short Hythes. Operations commenced in May 1947.

Initially the airline specialised in flying to attractive South Pacific destinations. Most enduring of these was their route from Sydney to Lord Howe Island which increased to six flights per month in 1949 and remained a staple throughout the airline's life. Trans Oceanic also flew charters and unscheduled services to Noumea, New Hebrides and the Solomons, but these declined due to lack of demand.[11]

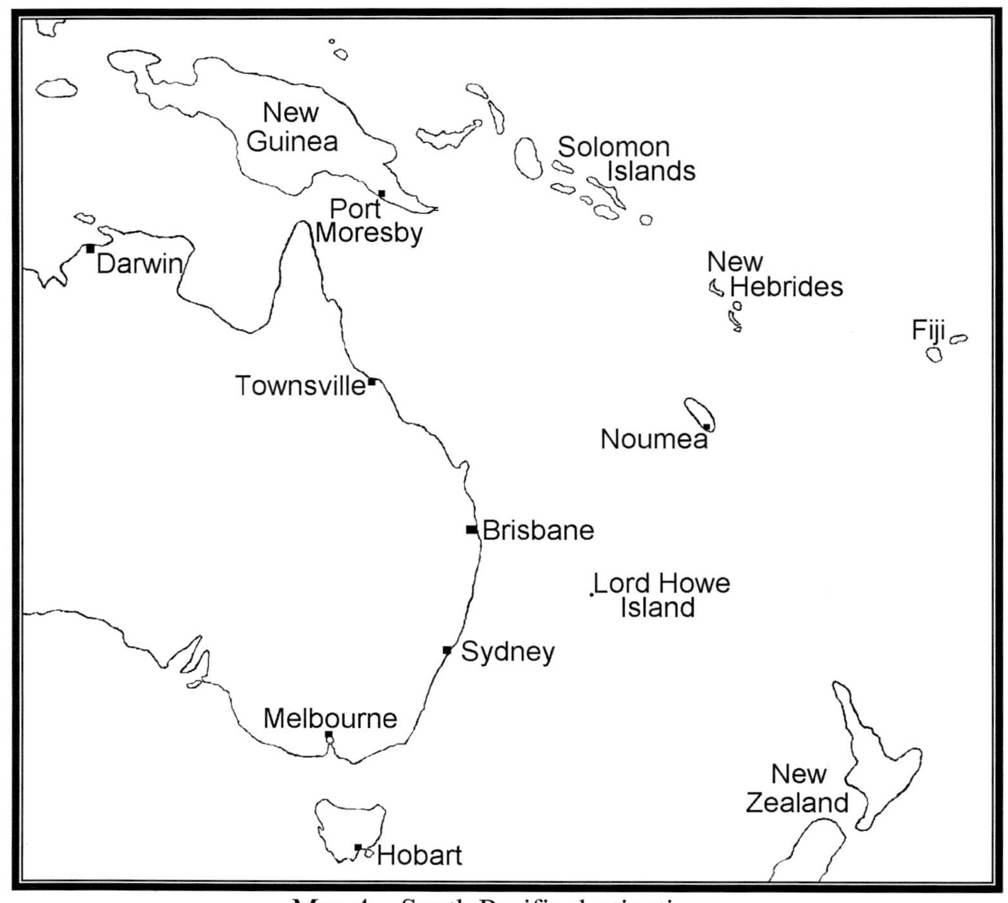

Map 4 – South Pacific destinations

While flights to the north-eastern islands had ceased by the beginning of 1951, other routes were developed south to Hobart and north to New Guinea. In addition, the airline bought a fleet of Short Solents from BOAC. These were the last word in civil flying boat design, faster than the Sandringham and carrying 40 passengers in comfort. Trans Oceanic's first Solent was delivered to Sydney on 4 April 1951 after calling at Brisbane earlier that day.[12]

The New Guinea service introduced Brisbane into Trans Oceanic Airways' route network. Barrier Reef Airways was appointed the airline's agents in Brisbane and managed local airport handling. Planned as a weekly service from Sydney to Port Moresby, the first departure for New Guinea took place on 29 October 1950 when the Hythe *Pacific Star* passed through Brisbane. Although only two passengers were aboard, Trans Oceanic was upbeat about their prospects. There was a "healthy booking" for the return flight and high hopes were held that the service would multiply to twice daily within five years.[13]

It was a long and demanding journey. Leaving Sydney on Sunday morning, the flying boat touched down at Hamilton just before midday and continued on to Townsville where it stopped overnight. The journey continued next morning to arrive in Port Moresby around lunch time. The return flight from Port Moresby to Sydney on Tuesday took just one day. Townsville was omitted from the southbound schedule resulting in a non-stop leg of 8½ hours from Port Moresby to Brisbane.[14]

But the euphoria of the first New Guinea flight did not last. The second service a week later was cancelled due to rough seas at Townsville. The service was discontinued pending the arrival of the airline's Solents which could fly from Brisbane to Port Moresby non-stop.[15]

When the faster Solents arrived, the weekly Sydney-Port Moresby service was reinstated as their "Chieftain Service". The new service was inaugurated in style on 27 May 1951. All seats aboard the Solent *Star of Papua* were filled by invited guests including a full contingent of press reporters. Hosting the party was one of Trans Oceanic's directors, Captain P.G. Taylor, newly returned from his triumphant South Pacific crossing.[16]

The Chieftain Service was streamlined to cut the overall return time in half. Instead of the Hythe's three day round trip with two overnight stops, the Solents left Rose Bay at 7.15pm of a Sunday night, flew through the night to arrive at Port Moresby at 6.30am the following morning. Three hours later the Solent took off on the return flight touching down in Sydney around 8.15pm.[17] The early arrival in Port Moresby provided a further day's saving for passengers connecting with morning services to Lae which had to cross the Owen Stanley Range before cloud descended to prevent further flying.

Townsville was removed from the schedule and Brisbane was the Solent's only intermediate stop in both directions. It was a more efficient use of aircraft and a more attractive timetable for travellers. After a second Solent was delivered, the schedule was doubled to two flights a week departing Sydney on Sundays and Wednesdays.[18] But the overnight flight north involved a night landing at Hamilton, taking off around midnight for the seven hour stage to Port Moresby. This was the first scheduled service to use the Brisbane River at night and it had drawbacks.

Trans Oceanic Airways Solent *Star of Papua* at Colmslie, having just arrived after a long day's flight from Port Moresby. (*Courier Mail* photo via John Wilson)

Predictably, the engine noise at midnight drew complaints from local residents. But more serious still, night-time movement of flying boats at Hamilton heightened the risk of accident. This reinforced the Harbour Master's oft-expressed concerns that seaplanes on the river were a marine hazard. Two serious accidents in 1951 proved these concerns were justified and gave urgency to the search for a safer location for the water airport. The first occurred on only the Solents' fourth Chieftain Service.

Star of Papua arrived at Hamilton to refuel at 10pm on 18 June and two hours later was ready to leave with eight passengers and nine crew on board. Just before midnight the DCA control launch sighted a vessel approaching the eastern end of the take-off area. This was the 50 tonne fruit boat *Florant* which the control launch intercepted, directing her to the north shore to pass outside the flare path.

While this was taking place *Star of Papua* began starting her engines and slipped her moorings. But as she moved out, two of her engines failed to fire and the flying boat made a wide swing across the river towards its northern shore. Here *Florant* was pressing so close to the bank that she was touching bottom.[19] The control launch immediately sent a radio warning to the Solent alerting her to the dangerous situation ahead of her, but no reply was received. The warning was repeated three times, but each time without an answer.

The Solent continued to bear down on the two small vessels and by the time her crew saw them a collision was inevitable. *Star of Papua*'s operating engines were cut and the strong out-going tide drove her into the *Florant*, stoving in the flying boat's nose and slightly damaging the fruit boat. The current swept the Solent on into the northern rock wall of the river and a nearby wharf where further damage was sustained by her starboard wing. The whole drama had taken place in under four minutes.[20] Fortunately no one was hurt, but repairing damage to the *Star of Papua* cost £10,000 before she returned to service.

By a cruel irony, *Star of Papua*'s pilot was Captain P.G. Taylor, who two months earlier had brought *Frigate Bird II* home from its pioneering flight to South America, and more recently had been the showpiece for the opening of Trans Oceanic's Chieftain Service.

The bow of Solent *Star of Papua* damaged in her collision on 19 June 1951.
(NAA Melbourne: B638, 410/5/29)

The DCA investigation found the accident was caused by the Solent crew's not keeping a listening watch on their radio either before or after moving from their mooring.[21] Captain Taylor protested strongly against these findings. While admitting to leaving the moorings before radio contact was made he described the cause of the collision as;

> "The use by Trans Oceanic Airways of an unserviceable aircraft, and the licensing for night operation by the D.C.A. of a base over which it had no control of traffic, except aircraft; ... which together caused me to start my engines and slip the mooring to make radio contact with the Tower."

He concluded "night operations should not be permitted in any part of the Brisbane River unless and until the D.C.A. has direct control of all traffic in the base area."[22]

His feelings at the time of this letter had been strengthened by a second and even more serious accident four months after his own. This accident involved another Solent, *Star of Hobart* (Captain P.H. Mathieson) with ten passengers aboard, which struck the bucket dredge *Platypus II* during take off just before midnight on 28 October 1951.

For several weeks the *Platypus II* had been working her way upstream, deepening the shipping channel towards Hamilton. On 28th October she was anchored with riding lights burning off the southern shore of the river near the flying boat base. Her position was about 250 metres beyond the eastern end of the flare path. The accident that followed was the result of an unfortunate chain of events.

The *Star of Hobart* landed from Sydney at 10pm and was warned about the dredge and taxied around it in coming to her buoy. Departing an hour and a half later, the Solent taxied upstream against a strong ebb tide to take off eastwards. Captain Mathieson handed over command of the aircraft to another pilot who was then undergoing conversion to flying Solents.[23] Taxiing against an adverse tide, the aircraft was well short of the full length of the flare path when it commenced its take off run.[24] Furthermore, because of his inexperience in handling a Solent, particularly in countering its engine torque veering the aircraft to starboard, the pilot took longer than normal to become airborne.[25]

Suddenly Mathieson and the pilot saw the lights of the dredge in front of them, but there was not enough room to avoid and the Solent's starboard wing hit the dredge's superstructure. 6.7 metres of the wing was torn off and the flying boat swung around and skidded into the mud on the southern bank of the river, fortunately without anyone being hurt.[26]

Blame for the *Star of Hobart* accident was argued in the High Court with both sides believing they had a strong case. Finally in 1956 Justice Williams handed down his judgment. Out of the diverse range of decisions and circumstances affecting that night's events the judge selected a single factor as cause of the accident. He considered the changing tide between when the Solent landed and took off had moved the flare path buoys on the slack of their moorings, placing the anchored dredge in the line of take off. On the question of shared responsibility he took a narrow view, laying blame solely on the DCA and assessing £31,000 damages.[27]

Star of Hobart rides to her moorings at Colmslie awaiting repairs for her damaged wing. This damage proved terminal for both the aircraft and the airline. (*Telegraph* photo via John Wilson)

Chapter 7 – Placed on Notice

"It will be necessary for the Queensland authorities to agree to a site which meets the practicable use of seaplanes.... Unless this action is taken the Commonwealth can see no way of meeting the State's wishes or providing safe conditions for aircraft."[1]

The consequences of the *Star of Hobart*'s accident on 28 October 1951 were profound. This was just the kind of calamity Brisbane's port authorities had warned about and the Queensland Government acted promptly. In a letter to the Prime Minister the Queensland Premier advised that the Hamilton Reach would be closed to night flying. He also announced that the site occupied by the Hamilton flying boat terminal had been leased for wharf development from the beginning of the next month.[2]

The ban on night flying from Hamilton, imposed initially by the DCA, could be overcome by laying a flare path in the downstream reaches of the river. But leasing the Hamilton property would have a more permanent impact. Arrangements in 1940 for the DCA's occupation of the Hamilton site had never been formalised. While this worked satisfactorily in the prevailing wartime environment, the situation was bound to be challenged subsequently by commercial pressures. Brisbane Stevedoring and Wool Dumping Coy Ltd, wanted to extend Hamilton Wharf and the lease enabled them to construct No.3 berth.

As if these setbacks were not enough, news now came through that plans for the flying boat base at Pinkenba had collapsed. The Department of Harbours and Marine rejected the proposed design because its pontoon and mooring buoys would encroach on the main shipping channel.[3] Also, wharf development at Pinkenba promised to replicate the traffic problems that were driving flying boats out of Hamilton. As 1951 ended prospects for flying boats remaining on the Brisbane River looked grim.

The *Star of Hobart* accident also proved costly for Trans Oceanic Airways. The damaged Solent was beached at Colmslie while the company searched the world for a replacement wing. None could be found and the aircraft was eventually scrapped.[4] But the *Star of Hobart* was just an added woe to what was already a bad year for Trans Oceanic. Rising running costs and increased competition from landplanes had taken a heavy toll of the airline which lost £100,000 on operations over the year. Such losses could not be sustained. With over £200,000 owing on the purchase of its Solent fleet, the Directors resolved on 30 June 1952 to place Trans Oceanic Airways into voluntary liquidation.[5]

1952 would be an uneasy year for flying boats in Brisbane as urgent efforts were made to secure their future in the area.

To overcome the ban on night flying from Hamilton, night operations moved downstream with flare paths being laid as appropriate in the Quarries, Pinkenba or Lytton Reaches of the river. Some inconvenience was suffered by increased time spent taxiing to the terminal which could take as long as half an hour.[6] Qantas preferred putting safety first and its flying boats avoided the Brisbane River after dark.[7]

Though the Hamilton terminal's days were numbered, DCA negotiated with Brisbane Stevedoring and Wool Dumping to keep the terminal in operation throughout 1952. In this period Barrier Reef Airways was its main user with flying boats moving on almost a daily basis. Qantas used the base less frequently, with their Port Moresby service passing through fortnightly in each direction. South Pacific flights alighted in Brisbane occasionally and the river was also used for emergency diversions.[8]

The Sandringham *Princess of Cairns* rests peacefully on a sunlit Hamilton Reach. (photo courtesy Ron Peterson)

With the collapse of plans for Pinkenba, DCA looked further afield to consider possible areas of Moreton Bay. But sites at Wynnum, Cleveland and Scarborough were considered, but these were dismissed due to their unprotected water. The only area of Moreton Bay considered suitable for flying boats was in the vicinity of Victoria Point, 42 kilometres from the city.[9] Here the waters of Redland Bay were protected by a circle of surrounding islands while offering long stretches of water free of competing marine traffic. The area was surveyed by the Department of Harbours and Marine in March and evaluated by both State and Federal Governments.[10]

Victoria Point was tentatively chosen for a shore base and plans were drawn up in 1952 for full flying boat facilities. These included a slipway, a shallow "nose hangar", terminal and aircraft hardstand on a small, man-made island joined by a 215 metre causeway road to the southern tip of Victoria Point.[11] But for £100,000, this ambitious scheme was considered too expensive and it went no further.[12]

While these events were being pursued, two further accidents took place at Hamilton. Both involved Barrier Reef Airways whose services out of Brisbane were growing.

Around 11pm on 11 July 1952 the loaded coal barge *Barrambin*, straying from the channel, struck the Sandringham VH-BRD (now named *Princess of Cairns*) as she lay at her moorings, damaging her port wing. Coming at the height of the tourist season with a full schedule of bookings to Hayman Island, this accident caused the airline considerable disruption.[13] The *Princess of Cairns* was out of action for a total of three and a half weeks while Catalina *Buccaneer* carried on alone.[14] To make up for the Sandringham's absence, Barrier Reef had to charter land based aircraft to fly passengers to Proserpine, completing their journey by launch.

But worse was to come three months later. At 2.20am on 31 October 1952, the captain of a passing dredge reported *Princess of Cairns* was in a sinking condition at her buoy.[15] Daylight showed her sitting on the bottom with only her fin, rudder and a wing tip showing above water. An unidentified vessel had struck her overnight putting a large hole in her port float. This caused her to list, water entered through a forward door and she foundered in 4.3 metres of water.[16] It took more than three days to raise and beach the flying boat, but salt water flooding had damaged her beyond repair and she was declared a total loss.[17] Once again the airline was reduced to just a single Catalina, and the Saturday-Sunday return service to Cairns was suspended.

Barrier Reef's other Sandringham had been out of service since early 1951 but a team of Ansett staff worked around the clock for seven weeks to bring it into operation in time to meet the heavy Christmas demand to Sydney. VH-BRC, now named *Beachcomber*, resumed passenger service on 21st December restoring the airline to its normal operating strength of two flying boats.

Between them, these two aircraft carried a record 2,500 passengers on the Brisbane-Sydney route between 15 and 30 December 1952.[18]

Salvaging *Princess of Cairns* on 3 November 1952. (Jack Richards via John Wilson)

This favourable position did not last for long as Catalina *Buccaneer* was grounded on 20 January 1953 with leaking fuel tanks. For the third time in six months Barrier Reef Airways was forced back onto a single aircraft to maintain its interstate and Great Barrier Reef services.

Buccaneer was repaired, but instead of returning to scheduled services, she embarked on a survey flight to help Reg Ansett evaluate some emerging business opportunities. At this time Trans Oceanic Airways was in liquidation and Ansett was considering its purchase along with the possibility of using flying boats for air cruises to the South Pacific. The Catalina left Brisbane on 17th February to survey a route for such cruises. Ansett and Stewart Middlemiss were on board and in a flight covering three weeks they travelled to Noumea, Western Samoa, Aitutaki in the Cook Islands, and Tahiti. By the time *Buccaneer* returned they had proved the feasibility of air cruises and these were introduced for the luxury market during the following years.[19]

But *Buccaneer* was becoming worn out, leaks in her hull having given trouble on her long Pacific voyage. With inspection to renew her airworthiness certificate due in three months time, repairs were considered uneconomic.[20] She was withdrawn from service, and all the airline's Catalinas were dismantled and melted down for scrap.

The retirement of Barrier Reef's last Catalina meant the airline could no longer service Heron Island. The main reason for creating Barrier Reef Airways in the first place had been to save Heron Island's guests the ordeal of a long and uncomfortable boat trip from the mainland. The airline had now been swallowed up in the Ansett conglomerate which had no business interest in Heron Island. Once more visitors to Heron Island faced a rough, 64 kilometre sea passage to reach their destination.

The damage, then loss of *Princess of Cairns* served only to underline what was already obvious to Barrier Reef Airways. The airline could not stay much longer at its Colmslie base. DCA plans for flying boat bases at Pinkenba and Victoria Point had evaporated and the airline needed a secure home if it was to continue in operation.

As over two thirds of its passengers for the Great Barrier Reef came from southern States, relocating to Sydney's Rose Bay was the natural solution.[21] With Trans Oceanic Airways under liquidation, Stewart Middlemiss quickly recognised the possibilities offered by their hangars at Rose Bay. On 16 August 1952 he wrote to the DCA asking that these hangars be made available to his airline.

The Regional Director in Brisbane strongly supported Middlemiss's plea and wrote to his Director General.

> "If it is your intention to proceed with the removal of flying boat activities from the Brisbane River to the Victoria Point site, it would appear that this can be achieved much more expeditiously and economically if accommodation is found for the Company [Barrier Reef Airways] at Rose Bay. This would mean that the new Base would require to be used as an itinerant alighting area only, resulting in a saving of a considerable sum of money for the slipway and hangar accommodation."[22]

It was a compelling argument that would not be lost on the bureaucrats. Barrier Reef Airways entered into negotiations with Trans Oceanic's liquidators, but the price being asked was too high for Middlemiss to accept, and the hangars were still being used as 1952 ended.[23]

Then on 13 January 1953, the Minister for the Army, Sir Jos. Francis, who was also local MHR for the Redlands area, announced that Brisbane's water airport would move from Hamilton to Redland Bay by July. The new base would be a "working skeleton" expected to cost only £4,250.[24]

This news alarmed Middlemiss who thought the change "would kill the business".[25] Without any maintenance base proposed for Redland Bay and nothing yet available at Rose Bay, in six months time Barrier Reef Airways would be stranded. Middlemiss complained his airline had failed to receive any assistance from DCA in providing facilities at either airport and moving out of the Hamilton Reach would prove very costly without Government help. A week later a ray of hope glowed as negotiations commenced with Qantas for Barrier Reef Airways to share their servicing facilities at Rose Bay.[26]

These negotiations never reached a conclusion. Trans Oceanic Airways finally agreed on a price for the sale of its assets, and on 20 May 1953, Ansett bought its Sydney properties, its route network and one of its aircraft.[27] The assets included Trans Oceanic's marine base at Rose Bay which was now available as a home for Barrier Reef Airways' aircraft. Middlemiss later called it a "godsend".[28] Indeed it was as Hamilton flying boat base closed down just two weeks later.

Other changes accompanied the move to Sydney. Barrier Reef Airways had been part of the Ansett group for three years. Now the airline was fully integrated as Ansett Flying Boat Services and the name Barrier Reef Airways disappeared into history. The route network purchased from Trans Oceanic Airways added Lord Howe Island and Hobart to Ansett's existing services from Sydney via Brisbane and the Whitsundays to Cairns.

The purchase included Trans Oceanic's Hythe, *Tahiti Star.* This aircraft joined Barrier Reef's surviving Sandringham, *Beachcomber*, to restore the fleet once more to two aircraft. Based in Sydney, *Tahiti Star* took over the Monday and Friday return service to Brisbane from 1 June 1953 in addition to its Lord Howe Island run.[29] Ties with the Brisbane River were finally cut on 6 November 1953 when Ansett terminated the Colmslie lease and handed the land back to the Army.[30]

Chapter 8 – Redland Bay

"Redland Bay was the only area with the necessary length of run and protective water suitable for the establishment of a water airport. It is approximately 26 miles from Brisbane ... but it is chosen in the absence of any nearer alternative site."[1]

Following the public announcement on 13 January 1953, the Prime Minister formally advised the Queensland Premier of Redland Bay's selection as Brisbane's new flying boat base.[2] After eight years of correspondence at the highest level of State and Federal governments a solution to the vexed question of flying boats on the Brisbane River had finally been found. It was not before time, as wharf construction at Hamilton had reached an advanced stage and would soon interfere with operations from the river.

In February plans for alighting strips, navigational aids, mooring and embarkation areas were submitted to the Harbours and Marine Department for approval. The plans provided for three alighting channels. Two of these, the main Snipe Island strip and the Pannikin Island strip at its southern end, were each over 3 kilometres long, half as long again as any land airstrip in Queensland. Heading north-east at the northern end, the Victoria Point strip was 2.1 kilometres long.[3]

The channels were each 150 metres wide and defined by permanent marker buoys. There would be three aircraft mooring buoys and further moorings for tender launches. An embarkation gangway and pontoon were installed off the south-eastern end of Redland Bay's jetty which had been strengthened and remodelled for use by DCA. A rotating light beacon and non-directional radio beacon would be erected on shore to help aircraft locate Redland Bay's flare path in both good and bad visibility.[4]

At the time of the Prime Minister's letter no arrangements had been made to secure land for the base at Redland Bay. Within two weeks an urgent request was sent to Redland Shire Council which quickly responded by offering twelve months permissive occupancy of six allotments on Banana Street. This was promptly accepted.[5] The rotating light beacon and two 21.3 metre masts for the homer beacon aerial were erected on this land.

But there were impediments for transferring foreshore property to DCA. This land had been reclaimed and filled using a State Government loan and subsidy, and negotiations involved all three levels of government. In the end the Commonwealth compulsorily acquired the full parcel of land, totalling .7942 hectares in August 1954, over 14 months after flying operations commenced at Redland Bay.[6]

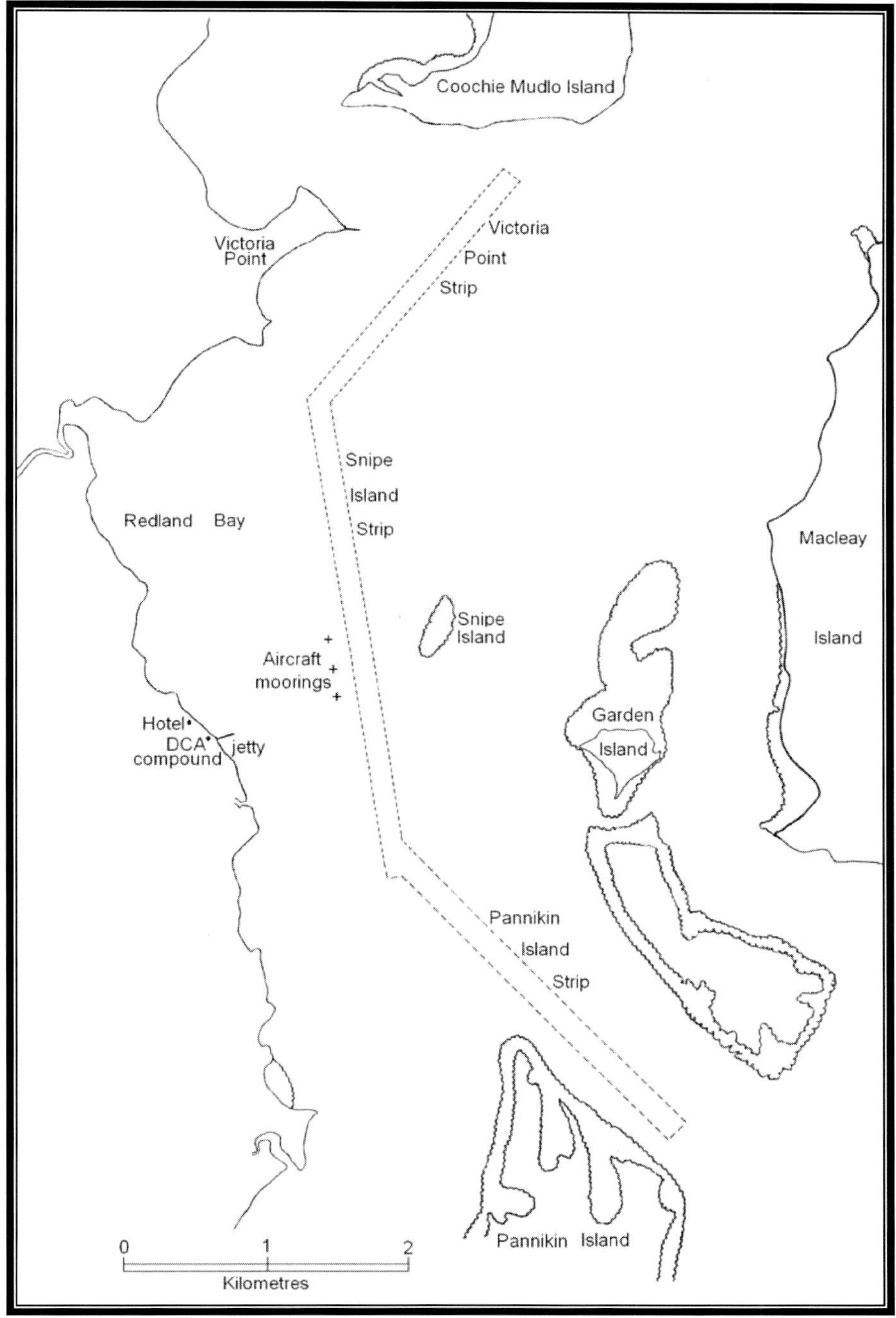

Map 5 – Redland Bay water airport

Plans had already been drawn up for the DCA's compound. In addition to the light and radio beacons it included an 18.3 metres by 6 metres control building for offices, store and workshop, as well as separate buildings for an inflammable store and buoy storage. Shell Company's oil storage tank was also located in the compound.[7] These plans were subject to revision, and delay as the DCA's head office baulked at the estimated cost of £6075. The buildings were not actually completed until 3 November 1954.[8]

Qantas, meanwhile, had recognised the need to provide comfortable passenger handling facilities and made its own arrangements with S. Sheldon, proprietor of the Redland Bay Hotel. The airline maintained a small office in the hotel for two years, and passengers awaiting flights could use its hospitality. As well as assisting the airline, the hotel also accommodated customs and immigration facilities and provided temporary accommodation for DCA staff until their own buildings were completed.

Detailed operational procedures were drawn up and published on 25 May 1953. Formal advice was also issued that Brisbane's water airport was being transferred to Redland Bay.[9]

Redland Bay jetty in the 1950s showing the embarkation pontoon, battery and flare storage shed, overhead lighting and launch moorings installed by DCA for the flying boat base. (photo courtesy Merlean Black and the Redland Shire Local History Collection (HP1051))

On 1st June a DCA launch cruised from Hamilton to Redland Bay and laid a flare path to test operational procedures at the new water airport. That evening Qantas Sandringham *Pacific Warrior* arrived from Sydney for a pilot familiarisation flight and carried out a series of night circuits and bumps at Redland Bay. Though DCA still did not have the land and buildings it needed on shore, the Redland Bay flying boat base was ready for business.

Wednesday 3 June 1953, was a pivotal day for Brisbane's water airport. At 7.19am Ansett's Sandringham *Beachcomber* took off from Hamilton and later that morning the second DCA launch sailed for Redland Bay. Staff ceased duty at Hamilton at 2pm and the Brisbane River base was closed. An hour later Redland Bay Flying Boat Base was declared officially open and within two hours two flying boats had alighted. *Beachcomber* had returned with passengers from Sydney, and Qantas Catalina *Island Chieftain* had also arrived from Port Moresby and stayed overnight.[10]

Transferring the flying boat base to Redland Bay had been a major effort. Next day DCA's Regional Director in Brisbane, A.W. Doubleday, wrote "a very heart felt THANK YOU" to his staff. The change-over had been smoothly completed despite the short notice of instructions.[11]

Redland Bay flying boat base compound with radio and light beacon towers (left) and offices in the control building (right). (photo courtesy Merlean Black)

For Brisbane's travelling public the move to Redland Bay was a retrograde step. The flying boat terminal at Hamilton was only a short drive from the city and close to Eagle Farm airport, but Redland Bay was 42 kilometres away in a farming area well outside the greater Brisbane area. Qantas countered this by saying the distance to Redland Bay would be compensated by quicker handling of planes in an area free from shipping hazards.[12]

However, the opening of Redland Bay was a positive move for Qantas. Freed from the dangers of using Hamilton Reach after dark, they rescheduled their Sandringham services to improve efficiency. All their international flights would now leave Rose Bay at 7.30pm and call at Redland Bay around 11pm before continuing their journey through the night. This would eliminate expensive overnight stops at Cairns and Noumea allowing flights to Port Moresby, Suva and the New Hebrides to be completed in under 24 hours, saving a day's travel on each route.[13]

Flying boat services to Port Moresby were increased to two a week enabling Qantas to withdraw the smaller DC3s from the route. The Bird of Paradise service would now be operated exclusively by four engine aircraft; Sandringham flying boats and DC4 Skymaster land planes. Routing their weekly flights to Suva and the New Hebrides through Redland Bay allowed the Sandringhams to embark Brisbane traffic and carry a greater payload to South Pacific destinations.[14]

The first outbound Qantas service using the new night schedule through Redland Bay was their Sandringham *Pacific Explorer* which arrived from Sydney a quarter of an hour before midnight on Monday 8th June. Two hours later she was back in the air bound for Noumea, where her passengers went ashore for breakfast.[15] Before lunchtime she had reached Vila in the New Hebrides, completing her journey in Espiritu Santo 1¼ hours further on. Thereafter Qantas Sandringhams made midnight calls at Redland Bay four times a week on their outbound runs to Port Moresby, Suva and the New Hebrides. Redland Bay residents soon learnt to recognise when a flying boat was due in at night. The powerful light beacon would be switched on, control launches began sweeping the alighting area, and local people would gather to watch the aircraft's arrival.[16]

Two southbound flights from New Guinea stopped at Redland Bay on a Friday and Saturday afternoon. Friday's flight originated in Rabaul the day before, but that on Saturday made the full journey from Port Moresby to Sydney in a single day with 13½ hours in the air. Homeward flights from Noumea continued to by-pass Brisbane, being routed directly to Sydney.[17] Flying west gave these aircraft the advantage of ending their journey in a later time zone, and night landing facilities at Rose Bay allowed the full trip from Suva or Espiritu Santo to be completed in a single day.

Qantas Sandringham *Pacific Warrior* takes off from Redland Bay for Noumea in July 1953. (*Courier-Mail* photo via John Wilson)

For Ansett Flying Boat Services, formerly Barrier Reef Airways, it was business as usual. This was the height of the tourist season and *Beachcomber* flew to Hayman Island each Sunday and Tuesday, the Tuesday flight originating in Sydney. Each Friday she flew from Redland Bay via Hayman Island and Townsville to Cairns, returning next day. The Hythe *Tahiti Star* maintained the regular connection with Sydney via Southport and Grafton every Monday and Friday. With the exception of *Beachcomber*'s return from Hayman on Tuesday evening, all Ansett's movements were in daylight.[18]

By July 1953 flying at Redland Bay had reached its peak with 105 commercial flying boat movements during the month and another 98 in August.[19] A passenger on one of these August flights was Tom Nunan, who flew to Fiji with the Australian Rugby Development Team. He remembers the trip.

> "Flying was still an adventure then and … we were issued with a red Qantas Travel Bag. We travelled to the small Qantas Office in Creek Street where the luggage was weighed and handed over and we were weighed individually. We were then taken to Redland Bay by car; … Redland Bay in those days was

the bush to anyone living in Brisbane and we seemed to take a long time getting there. The Sandringham Flyingboat arrived from Sydney with the New South Wales members of the team and we took off for Noumea at about 2350 hours. Passengers were treated with attention in those days and my impression of the Sandringham was comfortable seats, plenty of room and the ability to move around freely inside the craft. … I have had many flights since then but nothing can match the charm and comfort of the Flyingboat."[20]

Experience showed that the waters of Redland Bay were generally benign. But not always. Strong westerly cross winds and choppy seas caused the base to be closed three times during its first three months.[21] By contrast, an unruffled, glassy surface also created difficulties as surface tension held a loaded flying boat back from gaining enough speed to unstick. On these occasions the DCA launch surged ahead, creating a wake which broke up the sea surface, enabling the flying boat to lift off.[22]

****

Over the following months the frequency of services gradually fell. Ansett's flights to the Barrier Reef were wound back at the end of the winter tourist season and one of Qantas's weekly New Guinea flights was reduced to fortnightly. In March 1954 Ansett withdrew their ageing *Tahiti Star* from service and removed Grafton and Southport from their schedule.[23] Tourist runs to Hayman Island continued through the high season with their remaining flying boat, *Beachcomber.*

Towards the end of 1954 the DCA finally secured their land at Redland Bay and completed their service buildings. By then it was apparent that future use of the base would be limited. Qantas had reduced their flying boat services through Brisbane and planned to abandon them during 1955. Against this, Ansett indicated they would resume tourist flights to the Barrier Reef through the 1955 winter. They had also bought another Sandringham from Qantas, *Pacific Chieftain*, and planned to recommence operations between Sydney and Grafton.[24]

Qantas ceased international flying boat services in June 1955, retaining only a pair of Catalinas for internal flights in New Guinea. In their final months only two Qantas Sandringham services were scheduled through Redland Bay, a fortnightly return service to Port Moresby and an outbound flight to Fiji passing through each Wednesday night. The last Qantas flying boat to use Redland Bay was their Sandringham *Pacific Voyager* which took off on 21 June 1955 in the airline's concluding seaplane service from Port Moresby.

As Qantas was paying off its Sandringhams, Ansett was fully engaged with its winter tourist schedule to Hayman Island which commenced in May. This involved a northbound flight from Sydney via Redland Bay to Hayman Island each Saturday, returning to Sydney later that day or the next. In mid July these were stepped up by having the aircraft return to Brisbane on the Saturday evening to carry a second load to Hayman next day. The Sandringham came back through Redland Bay to Sydney later on the Sunday night.[25]

Ansett Sandringham *Pacific Chieftain* on moorings at Redland Bay in 1955 takes on fuel from 44 gallon drums aboard the contract launch *Tasma* owned by local resident Alf Hatchman. (*Courier-Mail* photo via John Wilson)

Redland Bay played a useful secondary role as emergency airport for flying boats diverted from Rose Bay. Possibly the most dramatic case occurred early in 1955 when Rose Bay was closed due to adverse weather. *Beachcomber* was then approaching Sydney on a flight from Hobart. She was forced to continue on to Redland Bay and arrived in darkness after 9½ hours in the air.[26]

Nevertheless, the decline in commercial flights through Redland Bay in 1955 caused the DCA to review its level of service. Maintaining three alighting channels was proving difficult due to silting, and in August two were closed, with just Snipe Island strip remaining open for a reduced length of 2,680 metres.

The annual running cost of £11,287 could not be justified after Ansett's tourist schedule finished in October and DCA proposed reducing some of its services.[27]

Stewart Middlemiss, writing on behalf of Ansett, objected to the closure of two alighting strips at Redland Bay. The remaining Snipe Island strip was unusable when a stiff westerly cross wind was blowing and a second strip was needed. He also argued that, while regular services to Hayman Island had finished, Redland Bay was the only alternative alighting area available should Rose Bay be closed for an emergency. Harking back to a theme used in his early days with Barrier Reef Airways, Middlemiss sealed his argument by complaining at the high level of fees charged by DCA and the service that was expected in return.

His arguments were ultimately effective. The Pannikin Island strip was reinstated in July 1956 in time for Ansett's tourist season flights into Hayman Island.[28] As in the previous year, these were scheduled from Sydney over the weekend involving some night landings, but they ceased with the end of the season on 6th October.

Ansett's use of Redland Bay declined in 1957 with their aircraft making only eleven visits during the whole year. Most were servicing Hayman Island, but one, arriving on 9th September, was from Noumea.[29] In addition to Ansett's regular route network, the airline ran three or four cruises a year to South Pacific destinations. Named "Carousel Cruises", these made a three week tour of Noumea, Fiji, Aitutaki and Tahiti. A week was spent in Tahiti which did not have a land airstrip at this time.[30]

When *Pacific Chieftain* took off on 17 September 1957 at the close of the season, it marked the end of Ansett's Sandringham service to Hayman Island.[31] Ansett had sealed Proserpine airstrip so their new Convair 340 airliners could fly into the Whitsunday area. In future tourists would fly in by these faster, pressurised aircraft with busses and launches completing the journey to their island resorts. Flying boat services through Redland Bay had ended and it seemed only a matter of time before the base would be closed.

Chapter 9 – The Lean Years

"They also serve who only stand and wait."[1]

After commercial flights through Redland Bay ended in September 1957, the base was kept only as a reserve for use in emergency by flying boats diverted from Rose Bay. As the years passed the base was scarcely used and maintaining it in operational condition came under question.

By 1961 its facilities were deteriorating and the pontoon was sold to save on repair costs. In addition, Shell had recently put its resident fuel barge up for sale. Faced with these realities and an annual running cost of £3,000, the DCA reviewed its activities at Redland Bay to consider whether the base should be closed.

Flying boat landings since regular services ended four years earlier were rare. Two Sandringham flights to Hayman Island called at Redland Bay during 1959, but one was an emergency when the aircraft developed engine trouble near Coolangatta. Then in November 1960 a new Ansett Catalina amphibian used for commuter flights between Proserpine and the Whitsundays made two publicity flights at Redland Bay.

However the review found Redland Bay was still in demand as a back-up for long distance flights. Between March 1959 and June 1961, Redland Bay staff were placed on stand-by for 36 different flights, mostly from Rose Bay to Noumea. But no diversions to Redland Bay actually took place on these occasions.[2]

DCA's review concluded that the Redland Bay base should be retained. But its facilities would be limited to just a single alighting strip, one mooring buoy and a single launch, reducing running costs to £550 per annum.[3]

Redland Bay settled down to a period of waiting, available should the need arise. Months of inactivity stretched into years, with just an occasional seaplane breaking the monotony.

One of these visits on 16 July 1962 brought Redland Bay briefly into the news. East Coast Airlines had bought a Grumman Mallard light transport amphibian for use on their tourist network. Still carrying its previous owner's Dutch New Guinea registration, JZ-POB, the Mallard alighted at Redland Bay for trials piloted by Captain Peter Ahrens.

Returning to Archerfield, a hydraulic fault disabled its undercarriage with one wheel locked down while the other two could not be lowered. After attempts to release the jammed undercarriage failed, the Mallard was escorted back to Redland Bay by another aircraft carrying the DCA Regional Director, R.M. Seymour, himself a former flying boat pilot. Under Seymour's guidance, Ahrens brought the Mallard safely down onto the water with full power on one engine counteracting the drag of the hanging undercarriage wheel.[4]

This aircraft was subsequently bought by TAA for use on their proposed "Coralair" service in the Whitsundays and was extensively refurbished at Archerfield. The Mallard conducted water tests at Redland Bay on 10 June 1963 for certification under its new registration as VH-TGA. But this service did not eventuate. The Mallard was found to be unsuitable for use in the weather conditions of Brampton Island and was sold to a New Zealand firm, leaving Australia on 12th October.[5]

After its emergency landing on 16 July 1962, the Grumman Mallard is drawn up on a boat ramp at Victoria Point for repairs. (photo courtesy Merlean Black)

By the early 1960s, Ansett had withdrawn from all flying boat routes except that to Lord Howe Island. Here the narrow, mountainous island was best served by flying boats landing on its lagoon. Ansett's two Sandringhams also undertook charters as opportunity arose. It was on such a flight, carrying delegates to a conference at Hayman Island, that one made an unscheduled visit to Redland Bay on 25 January 1963. The Sandringham could not land at Hayman due to rough seas and was forced to wait overnight. The conference was postponed 24 hours while the delegates were billeted in Brisbane hotels.[6]

Another charter taking bowlers to Fiji led to the loss of Ansett's *Pacific Chieftain* later that year. She broke adrift in a storm at Lord Howe Island and was damaged beyond repair. Left with only one aircraft, *Beachcomber*, to maintain Lord Howe Island's link with the world, Ansett sought a replacement. The search was difficult as large flying boats had disappeared from the air routes of the world. But the RNZAF provided the answer, selling one of their mothballed Sunderlands to Ansett. Converting it for civilian use and fitting it out as a Sandringham took many months. The new addition finally emerged as VH-BRF, *Islander*, making its maiden flight on 28 September 1964.[7]

****

Little changed for Redland Bay airport as the years dragged on. Few thought it would ever see more than the occasional emergency landing again. Then unexpectedly, in August 1965, instructions were received to make the base operational for flying boat services commencing in the following month.[8] A project to extend and renovate Gladstone airstrip was about to commence and the airport would be closed for several weeks. Queensland Airlines, an Ansett subsidiary, flew into Gladstone daily and their service would be disrupted during the construction period. Ansett's Sandringhams provided the solution, taking up once more one of Barrier Reef Airways' inaugural routes from 18 years before. Redland Bay was once more in the mainstream of flying boat activity.

Islander arrived on Sunday 12 September 1965 to start work next day.[9] The service operated every day except Sunday, departing from Redland Bay at 7.30am. Passengers could either assemble at Ansett-ANA's Eagle Farm terminal at 6am and travel to Redland Bay by coach, or meet on the jetty three quarters of an hour later. The journey took two and a half hours with return flights leaving Gladstone at 2.45pm during the week and noon on Saturday.[10] Gladstone's airstrip was re-opened four weeks later and *Islander* made her last return trip to Gladstone on 8th October.

Ansett Sandringham *Islander* rests at Redland Bay on 12 September 1965 before commencing a temporary service to Gladstone for Queensland Airlines. (photo courtesy John Wilson)

After an active month Redland Bay again settled back into a long period of waiting. The airstrip marker buoys with their wicker basket cladding remained in place defining an airstrip exactly one nautical mile (1.85km) long. Local sailors called it the "magic mile", sometimes using it for racing their craft.[11] A single caretaker kept basic facilities maintained. As well as mowing, painting, keeping light batteries charged and checking the buoys, his duties included taking the DCA launch for a monthly run to keep it operational.[12]

Throughout the 1960s the base's sole purpose remained to provide a refuge for flying boats on the Lord Howe Island route should Rose Bay be closed. In the event of an emergency, Redland Bay could be brought into operation at four hours notice, day or night, with staff from Eagle Farm airport.[13]

But emergency calls were rare and months turned into years until, quite suddenly, on Saturday afternoon, 19 July 1969, locals were surprised to see *Islander* (Captain R. Gillies) touch down on the waters of Redland Bay. A thick industrial smog had fallen over Sydney, closing Rose Bay airport and catching the Sandringham in the air on her way home from Lord Howe Island. *Islander*'s fifteen passengers were disembarked and bussed to Eagle Farm, completing their journey by airliner that evening.[14]

By the early 1970s the Lord Howe Island route was unique, the only flying boat service remaining anywhere in the world. Its veteran Sandringhams, now well over twenty years old, had become an attraction in their own right. In the twilight of their careers, the Sandringhams offered a last chance for people to relive or experience anew the romance of flying boat travel.

Islander lies at her buoy on 21 October 1971 before the last flying boat service out of Redland Bay. The jetty is in the background below Islander's tail while Redland Bay Hotel is among the trees on the right. (photo courtesy John Wilson)

It was to meet just such a request that a Sandringham made its final appearance at Redland Bay in October 1971. *Islander* was chartered by a group of aviation enthusiasts for a weekend flight to Lord Howe Island. Leaving Redland Bay on Saturday 23rd, the passengers enjoyed the natural beauty of lagoon and forest under the towering peaks of the island. Two days later *Islander* made the 800 kilometre homeward flight to Redland Bay. Disembarking its passengers the Sandringham took off at 5.15pm, made a low circuit, and returned to Sydney. This was the last time a flying boat ever used Redland Bay airport.[15]

By August 1971 the channel marker buoys were in poor condition, but any action to repair them was delayed pending an enquiry into the base's future.[16] The Sandringhams, too, were living on borrowed time. They were the only piston engined aircraft remaining in Ansett's fleet and had become uneconomic. During November 1972 Reg Ansett announced that the Sandringhams would be withdrawn within six months. He also criticised the lack of government action to build an airstrip on Lord Howe Island.[17] Environmental and cost considerations delayed any decision on the airstrip and the flying boat service was extended incrementally to meet the need.

Islander flies low in salute as she makes the final flying boat departure from Redland Bay on 25 October 1971. (photo courtesy John Wilson)

Finally, in March 1974, the Australian Army began building a runway on the island which was completed six months later.[18] The flying boats that had linked the island with the mainland for almost 30 years were paid off after their final flight on 10 September 1974. The surviving Sandringhams, *Islander* and *Beachcomber*, were sold overseas and left Australia later that year.[19]

The DCA reviewed its Redland Bay property in 1975 with a view to its disposal.[20] The radio beacon was still required for the safety of aircraft using Brisbane airport and continued in operation. The control building was occupied for a while by the CSIRO, then later by the Sea Cadets. Ultimately the buildings were dismantled and the property sold to Redland Bay Fishing Club.

Redland Bay itself hardly noticed the closure of its flying boat base. In 1957, the year regular air services into the bay ceased, a landing barge began using the beach at Redland Bay to load vehicles for ferrying to Stradbroke Island. An embarkation ramp was built near the jetty from which the *Myora* commenced regular car ferry services to Dunwich in 1964. Since then Redland Bay has become the bustling departure point for thriving communities on the southern islands of Moreton Bay.

Conclusion

It is now (2007) over half a century since flying boats operated from the Brisbane River and more than three decades since the Redland Bay flying boat base closed down. The nature of air travel has changed markedly and few remember flying boats on the Brisbane River. Brisbane's waterfront has changed so much that it has obliterated all trace of flying boat activity. The Domain where flying boats moored between the wars has been built out by the QUT and the Riverside Expressway. The flying boat terminals at Pinkenba and Hamilton have disappeared and been covered by wharf development.

At Colmslie and Redland Bay memories of flying boats may still be stirred. The site of the wartime American base later used by Barrier Reef Airways, has become Colmslie Reserve parkland, home of the Queensland State Hockey Centre. The current boat ramp is built on top of the base's beaching ramp, once used to bring large flying boats ashore. Shore facilities at Redland Bay were minimal and have since disappeared. But gazing out over the quiet expanse of water with its protective arc of islands, the qualities that made the bay ideal for flying boats can still be appreciated.

Memorials to remind us of these flying boats are few. A cairn at Brett's Wharf recalls the wartime arrival by RAAF flying boat at Hamilton of the first contingent of American airmen, and a plaque at Redland Bay Hotel commemorates that institution's flying boat associations.

Small amphibians and single engine seaplanes continue to operate tourist flights at the Great Barrier Reef and the Gold Coast. Just once, on 15 June 1983, a Grumman Turbo-Mallard amphibian landed on Hamilton Reach in a promotional exercise.[1] But even this nostalgic event happened over twenty years ago. The big flying boats have now receded into Brisbane's past. But in the few decades their wings graced the river, they wrote a colourful chapter in our city's history.

Chronology

1919 10 December, Ross and Keith Smith arrived at Darwin in first flight from Great Britain to Australia

1924 9 April, Goble and McIntyre arrived at Southport in first flight around Australia

1925 6 August, De Pinedo and Campinelli arrived in Brisbane in round flight from Italy

1928 9 June, Kingsford Smith arrived in Brisbane to complete first flight across Pacific Ocean

11/18 August, RAF Far East Flight of four flying boats in Brisbane from Great Britain

1937 21 December, Short Empire *Centaurus* arrived in Brisbane on route proving flight from Great Britain

1938 2 April, *Coolangatta*, Qantas's first international flying boat, arrived in Brisbane

5 July, Qantas commenced regular flying boat service from Australia to Great Britain

4 August, Empire Air Mail service between Australia and Great Britain commenced using Short Empire flying boats

1939 3 September, Second World War commenced and flying boat services reduced

1940 16 April, Brisbane's water airport moved from Pinkenba to Hamilton

19 June, Horseshoe Route introduced to Great Britain by-passing the Mediterranean

1941 8 December, Japan entered the war with widespread attacks in Southeast Asia and Pearl Harbor

1942 14 February, Qantas flights to Singapore ceased due to Japanese advance

9 September, U.S. Navy moved into property at Colmslie for a seaplane base

1944 6 December, U.S. Navy decommissioned its seaplane base at Colmslie

1945 4 October, Short Empire *Coriolanus* resumed peacetime flights for Qantas

1946 19 May, Qantas resumed flying boat services to Great Britain using BOAC Hythes

1947 12 July, Barrier Reef Airways began services from Brisbane to Gladstone, Heron Island and the Whitsunday Islands

1949 6 February, Qantas and BOAC withdrew flying boats from England-Australia route

1950 April, Sandringham flying boats added to BRA and Qantas fleets

3 July, Hayman Island resort opened by Ansett and added to BRA route network

1951 20 April P.G. Taylor landed *Frigate Bird II* in Brisbane near end of first return flight from South America

27 May, Trans Oceanic Airways began flying boat services to New Guinea

1951 November, night flying operations from Hamilton Reach banned following two serious accidents

1952 1 May, Barrier Reef Airways taken over by Ansett, becoming Ansett Flying Boat Services

31 May, Ansett Flying Boat Services extended their route to Cairns

30 June, Trans Oceanic Airways placed in voluntary liquidation

July, Qantas began Sandringham flying boat services to New Guinea

25 July, Ansett flying boats began calling at Southport on flights to Sydney

1953 13 January, announced Brisbane's water airport to be moved from Hamilton to Redland Bay

3 June, Hamilton flying boat base closed and Redland Bay base opened

1955 21 June, Qantas ceased flying boat services in Australia

1957 17 September, Ansett ceased regular flying boat services through Redland Bay

1965 13 September, Ansett began four weeks of interim flying boat services from Redland Bay to Gladstone

1971 15 October, departure of last flying boat to use Redland Bay

1974 10 September, flying boat services to Lord Howe Island ceased, the last flying boats in Australia were subsequently sold, and Redland Bay base closed

Abbreviations and Glossary:

BOAC	British Overseas Airways Corporation (now British Airways)
BRA	Barrier Reef Airways
CoA	Commonwealth of Australia
CTL	constructive total loss
DCA	(Commonwealth) Department of Civil Aviation
D/G	Director General
D/S	District Superintendent
DoI	(Commonwealth) Department of the Interior
FBB	Flying Boat Base
H&M	(Queensland) Department of Harbours and Marine
HMAS	His/Her Majesty's Australian Ship
HMS	His/Her Majesty's Ship (Royal Navy)
KLM	Royal Dutch Air Lines
KNILM	Royal Netherlands Indies Air Lines
MHR	Member of the House of Representatives (Federal Parliament)
NAA	National Archives of Australia
NATS	(U.S.) Navy Air Transport Service
PM	Prime Minister of Australia
QAL	Queensland Airlines
QEA	Qantas Empire Airways (now Qantas Airways)
QSA	Queensland State Archives
QUT	Queensland University of Technology
RAAF	Royal Australian Air Force
RAF	Royal Air Force
RAN	Royal Australian Navy
R/D	Regional Director
RNA	Royal National Association, organisers of Brisbane's annual exhibition
RNZAF	Royal New Zealand Air Force
RSC	Redland Shire Council
TAA	Trans Australia Airlines
TEAL	Tasman Empire Airways Ltd. (now Air New Zealand)
TOA	Trans Oceanic Airways
USN	United States Navy
USNA	U.S. National Archives
USS	United States Ship
amphibian	a type of aircraft able to land and take off from both water and land
flare path	line of lights defining the landing or take off strip to be used by an aircraft at night

flying boat — a seaplane in which the fuselage consists of a hull that provides buoyancy in the water

Marsden Matting – perforated steel panels laid on the ground and fitted together to form a hard surface for building airstrips, etc in World War Two

Pan Am — Pan American World Airways (U.S. international airline)

seaplane — any aircraft that lands on and takes off from water

windsock — open sleeve flown at an airport to show the wind direction

Appendix 1 – Flying Boat Types seen in Brisbane

Name	Number of Passengers	Engines (no. x hp)	Cruising Speed (kph)	Range (km)	Wingspan (metres)	Length (metres)	All-up Weight (kg)
Curtiss Seagull	2	1 x 160	96	463	15.2	8.8	1,239
Fairey IIID seaplane	3 crew	1 x 375	150	885	14	11.3	2,231
Savoia S.16ter	2 crew	1 x 450	120	2,093	14.9	10	2,955
Supermarine Southampton	5 crew	2 x 500	134	1,240	22.9	15.6	6,910
Supermarine Seagull III	3 crew	1 x 450	120	322	14	11.3	2,571
Short Rangoon	5 crew	3 x 540	148	1,046	28.3	20.3	10,228
Short Singapore III	6 crew	4 x 560	169	1,610	27.4	23.2	14,300
Fairchild Amphibian	8	1 x 645	248	2,415	17.4	13.9	3,785
Short Scion (floatplane)	4	2 x 90	187	628	12.8	9.6	1,455
Saro London II	6 crew	2 x 1000	171	4,186	24.4	17.3	8,762
Supermarine Seagull V	3 crew	1 x 625	145	1,020	14	11.6	3,100
Saro Cutty Sark	3	2 x 120	137	483	13.7	10.5	1,750
Short S.23 Empire	16 to 24	4 x 920	265	1,223	34.7	26.8	18,411
Consolidated Catalina (RAAF)	9 crew	2 x 1200	209	6,440	31.7	19.5	15,956
Martin PBM-3R Mariner	20	2 x 1700	265	4,825	36	23.8	25,458
Consolidated Coronado	24 to 44	4 x 1200	284	4,825	35	24.2	30,344
Short Sunderland III	13 crew	4 x 1030	286	4,667	34.4	26	22,700
Short Hythe	16 to 36	4 x 1030	265	3,783	34.4	26	22,700
Consolidated Catalina (civil)	14 to 22	2 x 1200	209	4,081	31.7	19.5	16,547
Short Sandringham	30 to 43	4 x 1200	283	3,930	34.4	26.5	25,424
Short Solent	40	4 x 1690	380	3,525	34.4	26.8	35,400
Grumman Mallard	10	2 x 600	290	2,222	20.3	14.7	5,796

Appendix 2 – Flying Boat Airlines Serving Brisbane

Qantas Empire Airways

Flying Boat Routes:

Empire Air Route – Sydney via Brisbane to Great Britain; July 1938 to June 1940

Horseshoe Route – Sydney via Brisbane to Cairo and South Africa; June 1940 to February 1942

Kangaroo Route – Sydney to Great Britain; May 1946 to February 1949

South Pacific – Sydney via Noumea to Fiji and New Hebrides; November 1945 to June 1955 (via Brisbane Nov. 1945 to Dec. 1947, June to August 1952 & June 1953 to June 1955)

New Guinea – Sydney via Brisbane to Port Moresby; July 1952 to June 1955

Flying Boat Fleet:

Short S.23 Empires;

VH-ABA *Carpentaria* bought 6.38, sold to BOAC 8.42 (G-AFBJ, scrapped 1947)

VH-ABB *Coolangatta* bought 18.3.38, impressed by RAAF 26.7.40 (A18-13), returned 23.7.43, crashed, Rose Bay 11.10.44

VH-ABC *Coogee* bought 9.38, impressed by RAAF 8.6.40 (A18-12, crashed, Townsville 27.2.42)

VH-ABD *Corio* bought 10.38, sold to Imperial Airways 9.39 (G-AEUH, shot down, off Timor, 30.1.42)

VH-ABE *Coorong* bought 9.38, sold to Imperial Airways 9.39 (G-AEUI, scrapped 1947)

VH-ABF *Cooee* bought 20.4.38, sold to BOAC 8.42 (G-AFBL, scrapped 1947)

VH-ABG *Coriolanus* (ex BOAC G-AETV) bought 8.42, withdrawn 23.12.47 & scrapped

VH-ACD *Clifton* (ex BOAC G-AFPZ, ex RAAF A18-14) transferred 7.43, crashed, Rose Bay 18.1.44

VH-ADU *Camilla* (ex BOAC G-AEUB) bought 8.42, crashed, near Port Moresby 22.4.43

Consolidated Catalinas;

VH-EAW (ex RAAF A24-378) bought 17.8.47, destroyed in explosion, Rose Bay 27.8.49

VH-EAX (ex RAAF A24-372) bought 7.10.47, wrecked in gale, Lord Howe I. 23.6.49

VH-EBA *Island Voyager* (ex RAAF A24-303) bought 13.12.48, withdrawn 7.53 & scrapped

VH-EBC *Island Chieftain* (ex Island Airways VH-ALN) bought 31.12.48, withdrawn 11.11.58 & scrapped

VH-EBD *Island Patrol* (ex RAAF A24-371) bought 29.7.49, withdrawn 11.11.58 & scrapped

VH-EBU *Island Warrior* (ex Island Airways VH-BDQ) bought 25.11.49, withdrawn 11.52 & scrapped

Short Sandringhams;

VH-EBV *Pacific Warrior* (ex BOAC G-AHZD) bought 15.7.51, withdrawn 6.6.55 & scrapped

VH-EBW (ex TEAL ZK-AMB) bought 18.4.50, struck reef & sank, Vila 10.6.51

VH-EBX *Pacific Chieftain* (ex TEAL ZK-AMD) bought 13.4.50, sold to Ansett 10.12.54 (VH-BRE)

VH-EBY *Pacific Voyager* (ex BOAC G-AHZF) bought 12.51, withdrawn 5.7.55 & scrapped

VH-EBZ *Pacific Explorer* (ex BOAC G-AHZG) bought 15.7.51, withdrawn 23.6.55 & scrapped

Barrier Reef Airways

Flying Boat Routes:

Brisbane to Gladstone and Heron Island; July 1947 to May 1952

Brisbane to Whitsunday Islands; July 1947 to May 1952 (extended to Townsville in June 1951)

Brisbane to Sydney; July 1951 to May 1952

Flying Boat Fleet:

Consolidated Catalinas;

VH-BRA *Beachcomber* (ex RAAF A24-369) bought 8.10.46, withdrawn early 1951 & scrapped

VH-BRB *Buccaneer* (ex RAAF A24-364) bought 28.10.46, transferred to Ansett 1.5.52

Short Sandringhams;

VH-BRC *Coral Clipper* (ex TEAL ZK-AMH) bought 7.4.50, transferred to Ansett 1.5.52

VH-BRD *Capricorn*, *Princess of Cairns* (ex TEAL ZK-AME) bought 27.4.50, sank at moorings & CTL, Brisbane R. 31.10.52

Ansett Flying Boat Services

Flying Boat Routes:

Brisbane to Gladstone and Heron Island; May 1952 to January 1953

Brisbane to Hayman Island, Townsville and Cairns; May 1952 to September 1957 (Townsville until September 1953, & Cairns until September 1954)

Brisbane to Sydney; May 1952 to September 1957 (via Grafton from June 1952 & Southport from July 1952 until March 1954)
Sydney to Hobart; 1953 to c.1955
Sydney to Lord Howe Island; May 1953 to September 1974
Proserpine to Hayman Island; October 1959 to July 1962
Brisbane to Gladstone; September & October 1965

Flying Boat Fleet:
Consolidated Catalinas;
VH-BRB *Buccaneer* transferred from BRA 1.5.52, withdrawn 10.3.53 & scrapped
VH-BRI *Golden Islander* (ex US commercial) bought 10.10.59, sprung leaks & sank, Hayman I. 8.7.62

Short Sandringhams;
VH-BRC *Beachcomber* transferred from BRA 1.5.52, sold to Antilles Air Boats 28.11.74 (N158C)
VH-BRE *Pacific Chieftain* (ex Qantas VH-EBX) bought 10.12.54, wrecked in gale, Lord Howe I. 3.7.63
VH-BRF *Islander* (ex RNZAF NZ4108) bought 18.12.63, sold to Antilles Air Boats 25.9.74 (N158J)

Short Hythe;
VH-AKP *Tahiti Star* (ex TOA VH-AKP) bought 20.5.53, withdrawn 12.3.54 & scrapped

Trans Oceanic Airways

Flying Boat Routes:
Sydney to South Pacific charters via Noumea; mid 1947 to early 1951
Sydney to Lord Howe Island; May 1947 to April 1953
Sydney to Grafton; 1947 to June 1952
Sydney to Hobart; mid 1950 to April 1953
Sydney via Brisbane to Port Moresby; October 1950, & May 1951 to April 1952

Flying Boat Fleet:
Short Hythes;
VH-AKO *Australis*, *Australia Star* (ex RAAF A26-4) bought 3.4.47, withdrawn 19.12.50 & scrapped
VH-AKP *Antilles*, *Tahiti Star* (ex RAAF A26-5) bought 3.4.47, sold to Ansett 20.5.53 (VH-AKP)
VH-BKQ *Pacific Star* (ex RAAF A26-2) bought 3.4.47, withdrawn 28.6.51 & scrapped

Short Solents;

VH-TOA *City of London* (ex BOAC G-AKNO) bought 22.1.51, crashed & sank on delivery flight, Malta 28.1.51

VH-TOB *Star of Papua* (ex BOAC G-AKNP) bought 23.3.51, sold to South Pacific Airlines 1.5.53 (N9946F)

VH-TOC *Star of Hobart* (ex BOAC G-AHIV) bought 7.51, collision & CTL, Brisbane R. 28.10.51

VH-TOD *Somerset* (ex BOAC G-AHIO) bought 4.10.51, sold to South Pacific Airlines 1.5.53 (N9945F)

P.G. Taylor:

Pioneer return flight Australia to South America; 13 March to 21 April 1951, in Consolidated Catalina;

VH-ASA *Frigate Bird II* (ex RAAF A24-385) transferred 22.8.50, withdrawn 28.6.54 for later museum display

Sydney to South Pacific charter cruises; 1954-1958, in Short Sandringham;

VH-APG *Frigate Bird III* (ex BOAC G-AKCO) bought 4.11.54, sold to Reseau Aerien Interinsulaire in Tahiti 1958 (F-OBIP)

Chapter Notes

Introduction
1. Allen, with Sherman, *Scotty Allen*, p.116.

Chapter 1 – Pioneers and Goodwill Visitors
1. Cobham, Sir Alan, *Twenty Thousand Miles in a Flying-boat*, p.16.
2. Byrnes, *Qantas by George!*, pp.11-14.
3. Miller, *Early Birds*, pp.93-98 & 112-113.
4. *The Queensland Times*, 7 to 11 April 1924.
5. Parnell & Boughton, *Flypast*, p.51.
6. Brogden, *History of Australian Aviation*, p.91.
7. *The Courier Mail*, 7 August 1925.
8. Wixted, *The North-West Aerial Frontier 1919-1934*, p.17.
9. Winchester (ed.), *Wonders of World Aviation, Vol. 2*, p.665.
10. Thetford, *Aircraft of the Royal Air Force 1918-57*, pp.384-385.
11. Wixted, *The North-West Aerial Frontier 1919-1934*, pp.28-29.
12. *The Sunday Mail*, 12 August 1928.
13. Wixted, *The North-West Aerial Frontier 1919-1934*, pp.28-29.
14. Thetford, *Aircraft of the Royal Air Force 1918-57*, pp.384-385.
15. *The Courier Mail*, 29 September 1934.
16. USNA: Record Group 80-G, negative 410848, Map of Brisbane, 25 March 1942.
17. George Roberts (Qantas Heritage Collection), interview, 23 March 2006.
18. *The Courier Mail*, 7 March 1936.
19. *The Courier Mail*, 27 June 1938; & NAA Melbourne: MP113/1, VH/UVQ, correspondence 21 October 1938 to 28 December 1939.
20. Thetford, *Aircraft of the Royal Air Force 1918-57*, pp.366-367.
21. *The Courier Mail*, 3 October 1934.
22. *The Courier Mail*, 6 October 1934.
23. Thetford, *Aircraft of the Royal Air Force 1918-57*, pp.360-361.
24. *The Courier Mail*, 21 & 22 January 1938.
25. *The Courier Mail*, 26 January 1938.
26. Thetford, *Aircraft of the Royal Air Force 1918-57*, pp.360-361.

Chapter 2 – Flying Boats to Great Britain
1. Editorial in *The Courier Mail*, 5 July 1938.
2. Jackson, *British Civil Aircraft 1919-59 Vol 2*, p.244.
3. Fysh, *Qantas at War*, pp.47-49.
4. Fysh, *QANTAS at War*, pp.51-55.
5. *The Courier Mail*, 21 to 26 May 1936.
6. Hall, *Flying High*, p.201.
7. *The Courier Mail*, 22 December 1937.
8. 'Douglas Commercial Log', in *AHSA-Journal*, Vol.17, No.1, p.8.
9. Robert Blaikie (long time Brisbane resident), e-mail to author, 8 August 2005.
10. *The Courier Mail*, 24 December 1937.
11. *The Courier Mail*, 27-28 January 1938.
12. Fysh, *QANTAS at War*, p.63.
13. *The Sunday Mail*, 3 April 1938.

14. *The Courier Mail*, 4 April 1938.
15. *The Courier Mail*, 4 May 1938.
16. *The Courier Mail*, 10 June 1938.
17. QSA: PRV8438, "Layout, Soundings, Charts etc. for a Flying Boat Base on the Brisbane River".
18. *The Courier Mail*, 10 June 1938.
19. QSA: PRV14712-1-429.
20. Len Roberts (RAAF Sunderland pilot), interview with author, 21 April 2006.
21. *The Courier Mail*, 6 April 1938.
22. Fysh, *QANTAS at War*, pp.57 & 67.
23. *The Courier Mail*, 10 June 1938.
24. *The Courier Mail*, 6 July 1938.
25. QSA: PRV14712-1-429, Schedule for Flying Boat Service – Singapore/Sydney section (Running-in service).
26. Byrnes, *Qantas by George!*, p.118.
27. Fysh, *QANTAS at War*, pp.69-70.
28. *The Courier Mail*, 6 July 1938.
29. *The Courier Mail*, 5 August 1938.
30. Stackhouse, *...from the dawn of aviation*, pp.71 & 74.

<u>Chapter 3 – The War Years</u>

1. Federal Cabinet decision in *The Courier Mail*, 9 December 1941.
2. Stackhouse, *The Longest Hop*, p.13.
3. "Gateway to Victory" memorial, Brett's Wharf, Hamilton.
4. QSA: PRV14712-1-429, letter Qld Premier to PM, 11 May 1945; & *The Courier Mail*, 16 April 1940; and George Roberts (Qantas Heritage Collection), interview with author, 23 March 2006.
5. Riddell, *Catalina Squadrons, First and Furthest*, pp.24; & 28-29.
6. NAA Canberra: A705, 171/106/1514, undated memo to RAAF Divisional Works Office, Brisbane.
7. NAA Canberra: A11066, 6/5/13, Brisbane Area Weekly Intelligence Reports Nos.37 & No.44.
8. USNA: RG 71, Records of the Bureau of Yards and Docks, Bureau of Yards and Docks, *Defence-Aid Reciprocal Aid Review Board Report*, section 9 – item 52.
9. QSA: PRV8298-1-5, letter DoI to Qld Co-ordinator General, 21 November 1942.
10. USNA: RG 38, box 1408 P38A, Records of the Office of the Chief of Naval Operations, Commander Seventh Fleet, *Base Facilities Report, 15 September 1944* (revised 6 January 1945), & USNA: RG 71, *Defence-Aid Reciprocal Aid Review Board Report*, section 9 – item 52.
11. USNA: RG 38, box 1408 P38A, *Base Facilities Report, 15 September 1944* (6 January 1945).
12. McCollum, A.H., transcript of interview, pp.490-493.
13. Morison, *New Guinea and the Marianas, March 1944 - August 1944*, p.49; & <u>http://www.daveswarbirds.com/blackcat/</u> .
14. USNA: RG 38, box 1408 P38A, *Base Facilities Report, 15 September 1944* (6 January 1945), & NAA Canberra: A11066, 6/5/13, Brisbane Area Weekly Intelligence Reports No.56.

15. USNA: RG 71, *Defence-Aid Reciprocal Aid Review Board Report*, section 9 – item 52.
16. NAA, Canberra, A705, 171/106/1514, Hamilton, RAAF FBB – Disposal of Surplus Assets.

<u>Chapter 4 – Return to Peace</u>

1. Fysh, *Qantas at War*, p.200.
2. "Qantas", in *Airplane* vol.2, no.19, p.506.
3. QEA timetables #25 15 Jan.'47 & #27 12 Feb.'47, courtesy Qantas Heritage Collection.
4. "Qantas", in *Airplane* vol.2, no.19, p.506.
5. NAA Brisbane: BP292/1, 214/108/1 Part 1, DCA memos 17 January, 21 July, & 28 November 1947.
6. Fysh, *Wings to the World*, p.18.
7. QEA timetables #25 15 Jan.'47 & #27 12 Feb.'47, courtesy Qantas Heritage Collection.
8. Stackhouse, *The Longest Hop*, p.47.
9. Alexander Frater (travel writer) & William Davis (BOAC steward) in video *From Sea to Sky*.
10. *The Courier Mail*, 10 & 18 May 1946.
11. QEA timetable #43 1 Dec.'47, courtesy Qantas Heritage Collection.
12. Jackson, *British Civil Aircraft 1919-59 Vol 2*, pp.119 & 249.
13. QSA: PRV14712-1-429, BCC letter to Dept of H&M, 24 September 1945 with map.
14. NAA Brisbane: BP292/1, 214/108/1 Part 3, map BS-11-X of Hamilton FBB, November 1951.
15. NAA Brisbane: BP292/1, 214/108/1 Part 1, DCA memo, 6 October 1950.
16. QSA: PRV14712-1-429, letters Qld Premier to PM, 11 May 1945 & PM to Qld Premier, 28 May 1945.
17. QSA: PRV14712-1-429, letters Qld Premier to PM, 22 August 1945 & PM to Qld Premier, 5 November 1945 & 16 April 1946.
18. QSA: PRV14712-1-429, letters Qld Premier to PM, 19 July & 9 August 1946, 21 May & 24 October 1947, 16 July 1948.
19. NAA Brisbane: BP292/1, 214/189/1 Part1, DCA memo 9 December 1946 & memo D/G DCA to Secretary PM Dept, 10 January 1951.
20. NAA Brisbane: BP292/1, 116/32/4, letter Minister for Civil Aviation to Hon J. Francis MHR, 5 October 1951.
21. NAA Brisbane: BP292/1, 214/108/1 Part1, letter Brisbane Portmaster to DCA, Eagle Farm, 14 July 1950.
22. QSA: PRV14712-1-429, letters Qld Premier to PM, 27 January 1950 & Brisbane Portmaster to BRA, 6 January 1949.
23. NAA Brisbane: BP292/1, 214/189/1 Part1, memo D/S DCA to D/G DCA, 21 January 1948.
24. NAA Brisbane: BP292/1, 214/108/1 Part 1, DCA letter, 13 January 1948.
25. NAA Brisbane: BP292/1, 214/189/1 Part1, memo D/G DCA to D/G Works and Housing, 20 April 1949 & memo D/G DCA to Secretary PM Dept, 10 January 1951.

26. NAA Brisbane: BP292/1, 214/189/1 Part1, telegram D/G DCA to R/D DCA, 12 December 1950.
27. NAA Brisbane: J56/11, QL2602, letter Qld Premier to PM, 7 September 1951.

Chapter 5 – Barrier Reef Airways

1. BRA magazine advertisement, courtesy Mrs Marion Eaton.
2. Banfield, 'The Stewart Middlemiss Story', in *Aviation Heritage*, vol.25, no.1, pp.16-17.
3. NAA Melbourne: MP347/1/0, 192/101/2081, item from *The Telegraph*, 2 July 1947.
4. NAA Brisbane: BP292/1, 014/6/6 Part 1, letter BRA to DCA, 13 June 1947.
5. Bartlett, 'By Air to the Reef', p.7.
6. Frank Kelly (BRA pilot), interview with author, 1 March 2006.
7. Frank Kelly interview with author, 1 March 2006.
8. Bartlett, 'By Air to the Reef', p.8.
9. Banfield, 'The Stewart Middlemiss Story', in *Aviation Heritage*, Vol.25, No.2, pp.29-30.
10. NAA Brisbane: BP292/1, 014/6/6 Part 1, letter BRA to DCA, 10 November 1947.
11. NAA Brisbane: BP292/1, 014/6/6 Part 1, letters BRA to D/S DCA, 2 June, 18 August & 23 December 1948.
12. NAA Brisbane: BP292/1, 014/6/6 Part 1, letter BRA to R/D DCA, 1 June 1950.
13. Mrs Marion Eaton (Daydream Island resident) interview with author.
14. NAA Brisbane: BP292/1, 014/6/6 Part 1, letters DCA to BRA, 7 May 1948, & BRA to DCA, 19 May, 2 June & 7 December 1948.
15. NAA Brisbane: BP292/1, 014/6/6 Part 1, letters BRA to DCA, 10 & 17 November 1947 & 22 December 1948.
16. NAA Brisbane: BP292/1, 014/6/6 Part 1, letter BRA to DCA, 6 April 1950; & Ludlow, *Moreton Bay Letters*, p.124.
17. NAA Brisbane: BP292/1, 014/6/6 Part 1, letters Com'r of Transport to D/S DCA, 28 September 1948 & BRA to DCA, 8 February, 12 & 15 December 1949.
18. Frank Kelly (BRA pilot) personal flying log book.
19. NAA Brisbane: BP292/1, 014/6/6 Part 1, letter BRA to R/D, DCA, 1 June 1950.
20. 1Barr, *No Swank Here?*, pp.38-39.
21. NAA Melbourne: MP347/1/0, 192/101/2081, letter BRA to D/G DCA, 30 June 1947.
22. NAA Brisbane: BP292/1, 214/189/1 Part 1, letter BRA to D/S, DCA, 28 December 1946.
23. NAA Brisbane: BP292/1, 214/189/1 Part 1, letter BRA to D/G, DCA, 5 July 1950.
24. QSA: PRV14712-1-429, letter Qld Premier to PM, 11 November 1949.
25. BRA brochure, courtesy Mrs Marion Eaton.
26. Frank Kelly (BRA pilot), interview with author, 1 March 2006.
27. Frank Kelly (BRA pilot) personal flying log book.
28. Banfield, 'The Stewart Middlemiss Story', in *Aviation Heritage*, Vol.25, No.2, pp.30-31.
29. Banfield, 'The Stewart Middlemiss Story', in *Aviation Heritage*, Vol.25, No.2, p.31.
30. Frank Kelly (BRA pilot), interview with author, 1 March 2006.
31. NAA Brisbane: J23/36, 1954/667 Part 1.
32. Banfield, 'The Stewart Middlemiss Story', in *Aviation Heritage*, Vol.25, No.2, p.31.

33. NAA Brisbane: BP292/1, 214/189/1 Part 1, letter BRA to D/G, DCA, 5 July 1950.
34. NAA Brisbane: BP292/1, 214/108/1 Parts 1 & 2, letter BRA to DCA, 20 September 1950, memo, December 1950, & memo Property Survey Branch, DoI, 24 August 1951.
35. NAA Brisbane: BP292/1, 014/6/6 Part 1, letter BRA to R/D DCA, 1 June 1950.
36. Frank Kelly (BRA pilot), interview with author, 1 March 2006.
37. NAA Brisbane: BP292/1, 116/35/2, letter DCA to BRA, 25 January 1951, & http://www.adastron.com/squawkid/squawk-1.htm#01JUL51
38. NAA Brisbane: BP292/1, 116/35/2, letter Dept of Transport to BRA, 20 November 1951, & QSA: PRV14712-1-429, memo R/D DCA, 9 April 1952.
39. QSA: PRV14712-1-429, DCA Air service Timetable No. 26A, 27 June 1952.
40. QSA: PRV14712-1-429, letters R/D DCA to Dept of H&M, 7 July 1952, & TOA to Dept of H&M, 25 June 1952 with DCA map BS-127-X.
41. *The Courier Mail*, 25 July 1952, & Banfield, 'The Stewart Middlemiss Story', in *Aviation Heritage*, Vol.25, No.2, p.32.
42. Wilson, *History of Civil Flying Boat Operations 1946-1974*.
43. NAA Brisbane: BP292/1, 116/35/2, BRA new timetable, 29 April 1952.
44. www.ansett.com.au/administrator/ansettatach1/milestones.pdf page 5.

Chapter 6 – Widening Horizons

1. Reflections of P.G. Taylor after an air battle in 1917 in Taylor, *The Sky Beyond*, p.17.
2. Taylor, *The Sky Beyond*, pp.357-358.
3. Fysh, *Wings to the World*, p.128.
4. *The Courier Mail*, 21 April 1951.
5. *The Courier Mail*, 26 May & 16 June 1951.
6. Allen, "The Short Flying Boats", in *Australian Aviation*, Sep 1982, pp.10 & 13.
7. Fysh, *Wings to the World*, pp.95 & 98.
8. NAA Brisbane: BP292/1, 214/108/1 Part 3, Qantas letter, 2 June 1952.
9. NAA Brisbane: BP292/1, 013/4/17 Part 3, Hamilton FBB log, 14 July 1952 to 3 June 1953.
10. Qantas timetable 1 Dec.'52 to 30 Jan.'53, courtesy Qantas Heritage Collection.
11. Croker, "Trans Oceanic Airways Pty Ltd", in *Aviation Heritage*, vol.23, no.1, p.15.
12. *The Courier Mail*, 5 April 1951.
13. *The Courier Mail*, 30 October 1950.
14. NAA Brisbane: BP292/1, 014/6/6 Part 1, memo officer in charge FBB Hamilton to R/D DCA, 19 September 1950 (dated 1951 in error; date stamps on letter, context & file order all indicate 1950).
15. Wilson, *History of Civil Flying Boat Operations 1946-1974*, p.8.
16. *The Courier Mail*, 28 May 1951.
17. QSA: PRV14712-1-429, memo R/D DCA to officers in charge of airports, 4 March 1952.
18. Wilson, *History of Civil Flying Boat Operations 1946-1974*, p.9.
19. John Wilson, letter to author of 29 October 2006 with notes from his interview with a deckhand of *Florant*.
20. NAA Melbourne: B638/22, 410/5/29, "Incident Report Aircraft VH-TOB", 19 June 1951.

21. NAA Melbourne: B638/22, 410/5/29, Report, DCA Inspector of Accidents, 14 December 1951.
22. NAA Melbourne, B638/22, 410/5/29, letter P.G. Taylor to D/G DCA, 15 September 1952.
23. NAA Canberra: A10072, 1952/19, Judgment TOA Ltd v. CoA, 21 September 1956.
24. E Jones (ex DCA) conversation with the author
25. NAA Canberra: A10072, 1952/19, Judgment TOA Ltd v. CoA, 21 September 1956.
26. Croker, "Trans Oceanic Airways Pty Ltd", in *Aviation Heritage*, vol.23, no.1, p.17.
27. NAA Canberra: A10072, 1952/19, Judgment TOA Ltd v. CoA, 21 September 1956.

Chapter 7 – Placed on Notice

1. NAA Brisbane: BP292/1, 214/189/1 Part 1, memo D/G DCA to Secretary PM Dept., 10 January 1951.
2. NAA Brisbane: BP292/1, 214/108/1 Part 3, letter Qld Premier to PM, 6 December 1951.
3. NAA Brisbane: J56/11, QL2602, letter Dept of H&M to DCA, 21 December 1951.
4. Croker, "Trans Oceanic Airways Pty Ltd", in *Aviation Heritage*, vol 23, no.1, p.17.
5. NAA Melbourne: B596, 422/48/16 Part 1, TOA Chairman's Report to Shareholders, 1 July 1952.
6. NAA Brisbane: BP292/1, 013/4/17 Part 3, Hamilton FBB log, 27 October 1952.
7. *The Courier Mail*, 14 January 1953.
8. NAA Brisbane: BP292/1, 013/4/17 Part 3, Hamilton FBB log, 14 July 1952 to 3 June 1953.
9. NAA Brisbane: BP292/1, 214/189/1 Part 1, memo R/D DCA to D/G DCA, 7 June 1951.
10. NAA Brisbane: J56/11, QL2602, R/D DCA memorandum, 13 May 1952.
11. NAA Brisbane: BP881/1, WH962, memo R/D DCA to Director of Works, Brisbane, 23 September 1952 with plans.
12. NAA Brisbane: BP292/1, 214/189/1 Part 2, letter R/D DCA to BRA, 31 October 1952.
13. *The Sunday Mail*, 13 July 1952.
14. NAA Brisbane: BP292/1, 013/4/17 Part 3, Hamilton FBB log, 14 July to 5 August 1952.
15. NAA Brisbane: BP292/1, 013/4/17 Part 3, Hamilton FBB log, 31 October to 4 November 1952.
16. Ludlow, *Moreton Bay Letters*, p.126.
17. *The Courier Mail*, 1 to 5 November 1952; & *The Sunday Mail*, 2 November 1952.
18. Wilson, *History of Civil Flying Boat Operations 1946-1974*.
19. NAA Brisbane: BP292/1, 013/4/17 Part 3, Hamilton FBB log, 14 July 1952 to 3 June 1953; and John Wilson (flying boat historian) letter to author of 29 October 2006.
20. Eyre, "Catalinas on the Great Barrier Reef", *AHSA Journal*, vol.14, no.4, p.64.
21. *The Courier Mail*, 23 January 1953.
22. NAA Brisbane: BP292/1, 014/6/6 Part 2, memo R/D DCA to D/G DCA, 19 August 1952.
23. NAA Brisbane: BP292/1, 014/6/6 Part 2, letter R/D DCA to BRA, 6 October 1952; and BP292/1, 214/189/1 Part 2, letter BRA to R/D DCA, 13 November 1952.

24. *The Courier Mail*, 14 January 1953.
25. Banfield, 'The Stewart Middlemiss Story', in *Aviation Heritage*, Vol.25, No.2, p.32.
26. *The Courier Mail*, 15 & 23 January 1953.
27. www.ansett.com.au/administrator/ansettatach1/milestones.pdf page 5.
28. Banfield, 'The Stewart Middlemiss Story', in *Aviation Heritage*, Vol.25, No.2, p.32.
29. NAA Brisbane: BP292/1, 013/4/17 Part 3, Brisbane FBB log, 1 June to 4 September 1953.
30. NAA Brisbane: J56/11, QL2602, Army advice, 30 April 1954.

Chapter 8 – Redland Bay

1. NAA Brisbane: BP292/1, 214/189/1 Part 2, letter Hon H.L. Anthony, Minister for Civil Aviation, to Rt Hon Sir Arthur Fadden, Treasurer, 30 April 1953.
2. QSA: Series PRV14712-1-429, letter PM to Qld Premier, 23 January 1953.
3. NAA Brisbane: J23/36, 1954/1285 Part 1, map BL 261Z attached to Operations Letter ATC 58/COM.32, 25 May 1953.
4. QSA: PRV14712-1-429, letter R/D DCA to Dept of H&M, 16 February 1953 & DCA Map HD-925W.
5. NAA Brisbane: J23/P11, 1957/946, letter DCA to RSC, 4 February 1953 & reply, 9 April 1953.
6. NAA Brisbane: J23/P11, 1957/946, CoA Gazette no.49, 12 August 1954.
7. NAA Brisbane: BP292/1, 216/15/2, letter R/D DCA to Director of Works, 13 April 1953.
8. NAA Brisbane: J23/P11, 1957/946, letter R/D DCA to DoI, 3 November 1954.
9. NAA Brisbane: J23/36, 1954/1285 part 1, Operations Letter ATC 58/COM.32, 25 May 1953, & BP292/1, 214/108/1 Part 3, Notam II No.64/1953.
10. NAA Brisbane: BP292/1, 013/4/17 Part 3, Hamilton and Redland Bay FBB logs, 1 to 4 June 1953.
11. NAA Brisbane: J23/36, 1954/1285 Part 1, Minute R/D DCA to Redland Bay FBB staff, 4 June 1953.
12. *The Courier Mail*, 14 January 1953.
13. "Sandringham Services Increase", in *Qantas News*, May 1953 No.5, & Qantas timetable, 14 Nov.'53, courtesy Qantas Heritage Collection.
14. Internal QEA memo "Notes on 1953 Statistics" dated 15 May 1954 in Sir Hudson Fysh papers, courtesy Qantas Heritage Collection.
15. NAA Brisbane: BP292/1, 013/4/17 Part 3, Redland Bay FBB logs, 3 June to 5 September 1953.
16. Merlean Black (Redland Bay resident), recollections in conversation with the author.
17. Qantas timetable effective 14 Nov.'53, courtesy Qantas Heritage Collection.
18. NAA Brisbane: BP292/1, 013/4/17 Part 3, Redland Bay FBB logs, 3 June to 5 September 1953.
19. NAA Brisbane: BP292/1, 013/4/17 Part 3, Redland Bay FBB logs, 3 June to 5 September 1953.
20. Nunan, Tom, e-mail of 2 January 2006.
21. NAA Brisbane: BP292/1, 013/4/17 Part 3, Redland Bay FBB logs, 3 June to 5 September 1953.
22. Graham Barnett (Redland Bay resident), interview with author, 2 June 2006.

23. Croker, "Trans Oceanic Airways Pty Ltd", in *Aviation Heritage*, Vol.23, No.1, p.16.
24. NAA Brisbane: J23/36, 1954/2586 Part 3, memos D/G DCA to R/D DCA, 9 February 1954, & R/D DCA to D/G DCA, 11 February 1955.
25. NAA Brisbane: J23/36, 1954/2586 Part 3, memo R/D DCA to D/G DCA, 28 February 1956.
26. NAA Brisbane: J23/36, 1954/2586 Part 3, letter Redland Bay FBB to R/D DCA, 17 August 1955.
27. NAA Brisbane: J23/36, 1954/2586 Part 3, DCA NOTAM II, 4 April 1955, & memo R/D DCA to D/G DCA, 12 October 1955.
28. NAA Brisbane: J23/36, 1954/2586 Part 3, letters Ansett to DCA, 26 September 1955 & 22 May 1956, & R/D DCA to Ansett, 22 June 1956.
29. NAA Brisbane: J23/36, 1959/428 Part 5, minute Airport Manager to R/D DCA, 7 June 1961.
30. Graeme Gillies (son of Ansett Sandringham pilot Ron Gillies), interview with author, 6 April 2006.
31. NAA Brisbane: J23/36, 1959/428 Part 5, minute Airport Manager to R/D DCA, 7 June 1961.

Chapter 9 – The Lean Years

1. John Milton, "On His Blindness".
2. NAA Brisbane: J23/36, 1959/428 Part 5, Minute Airport Manager to R/D DCA, 7 June 1961.
3. NAA Brisbane: J23/36, 1959/428 Part 5, memo R/D DCA to D/G DCA, 7 July 1961.
4. *The Courier Mail*, 17 July 1962.
5. Kelly (BRA & TAA pilot), note to author.
6. *The Courier Mail*, 26 January 1963.
7. Allen, "The Short Flying Boats", in *Australian Aviation* Sep 82, p.16.
8. NAA Brisbane: J23/35, 1970/2961 Part 1, file note, 24 August 1965.
9. *The Courier Mail*, 13 September 1965.
10. QAL timetable in http://www.adastron.com/squawkid/h2qaltt.htm .
11. John Moore (long time Redland Bay resident), interview with author, 9 June 2006.
12. Doug Lindsay (long time Redland Bay resident), interview with author, 8 June 2006.
13. NAA Brisbane: J23/35, 1970/2961 Part 1, Director of Public Relations, DCA message, 6 November 1968.
14. *The Sunday Mail*, 20 July 1969.
15. http://www.adastron.com/squawkid/squawk-1.htm#25OCT71 .
16. NAA Brisbane: J23/35, 1970/2961 Part 1, file note, 1 September 1971.
17. "Monthly Notes – Civil", in *AHSA Journal*, Vol. 13 No.6, p.81.
18. "Monthly Notes – Civil", in *AHSA Journal*, Vol. 15 Nos.1 p.14, & No.5 p.79.
19. Allen, Eric, "The Short Flying Boats", in *Australian Aviation* Sep 82, p.16.
20. NAA Brisbane: J56/11, QL2696, "Review of Commonwealth Land – Redland Bay – Department of Administrative Services (Queensland Branch)", 1975.

Conclusion

1. *The Courier Mail*, 16 June 1983.

Bibliography

Archives:

National Archives of Australia;

Canberra

Series No	Control Symbol	Title
A705	171/106/1514	Hamilton, Qld: RAAF Flying boat Base – Disposal of Assets
A10072	1952/19	Trans Oceanic Airways Ltd versus The Commonwealth of Australia
A11066	6/5/13	LDH and No.108 FCU – Weekly Intelligence Reports

Melbourne

B638	410/5/29	Accident VH-TOB at Hamilton 19 June '51
B596	422/48/16 Part 1	Trans Oceanic Airways liquidation proceedings
MP113/1	VH/UVQ	Short Scion S16/1 Aircraft VH-UVQ
MP347/1	192/101/2081	Barrier Reef Airways (S.C. Middlemiss)

Brisbane

BP292/1	013/4/17 Part 3	Reports, returns, statistics. Log – Redland Bay Flying Boat Base
BP292/1	014/6/6 Part 1	Routes – Barrier Reef Airways
BP292/1	116/32/4	Flying boat operation – Hamilton
BP292/1	116/35/2	Airline Licence Barrier Reef Airways – Ansett Flying Boat Service Pty Ltd
BP292/1	214/108/1 Parts 1-3	Hamilton Flying Boat Base [Parts 1-3]
BP292/1	214/189/1 Parts 1-2	Bases FB [Flying Boat]. Proposed base for Brisbane
BP292/1	216/15/2	Redland Bay FBB [Flying Boat Base] – Buildings
BP881/1	WH962	Proposed Flying Boat Base – Redland Bay – Site Investigation – Department of Civil Aviation
J23/P11	1957/946	Redland Bay Property
J23/35	1970/2961 Part 1	Redland Bay – Maintenance of alighting area
J23/36	1954/667 Part 1	Short Sandringham flying boat
J23/36	1954/1285 Part 1	Operations – Redland Bay
J23/36	1954/2586 Part 3	Redland Bay – alighting area
J23/36	1959/428 Part 5	Redland Bay – alighting area
J56/11	QL2602	Brisbane River – Flying boat base
J56/11	QL2696	Brisbane – Water Airport – Redland Bay
J1018/2	LS1446	Redland Bay – Radio
J1519	SP 3063/11	Australian Valuation Office – Redland Bay former Flying boat base

Queensland State Archives

Series	Title
PRV8298-1-5	Seaplane Base/US Navy – Brisbane River

PRV8438 Layout, Soundings, Charts, etc for a Flying Boat Base on the Brisbane River
PRV14712-1-429 Flying Boat Bases B1

U.S. National Archives

Record Group 38, box 1408 P38A, Records of the Office of the Chief of Naval Operations; Commander Seventh Fleet, *Base Facilities Report, 15 September 1944* (revised 6 January 1945).
Record Group 71, Records of the Bureau of Yards and Docks; *Defence-Aid Reciprocal Aid Review Board Report*, section 9 – item 52.
Record Group 80-G, 410848; Map of Brisbane, Australia, dated 25 March 1942.

Qantas Heritage Collection, Sydney

Qantas Timetables: #25 15 January 1947; #27 12 February 1947; #43 1 December 1947; timetable 1 December 1952 to 30 January 1953; timetable 14 November 1953.

Books:

Allen, G.U., with Sherman, Elizabeth, *Scotty Allen*, Clarion Editions, Balmain, NSW, 1992
Barr, T., *No Swank Here? The Development of the Whitsundays as a Tourist Destination to the Early 1970s*, James Cook University, Townsville, 1990
Brimson, Samuel, *Flying the Royal Mail*, Dreamweaver Books, Sydney, 1984
Brogden, Stanley, *History of Australian Aviation*, The Hawthorn Press, Melbourne, 1960
Byrnes, Paul, *Qantas by George!*, The Watermark Press, Sydney, 2000
Cobham, Sir Alan, *Twenty Thousand Miles in a Flying-boat*, Harrap, London, 1934
Driscoll, Ian H., *Flightpath South Pacific*, Whitcombe and Tombs, Christchurch, 1972
Eather, Steve, *Flying Squadrons of the Australian Defence Force*, Aerospace Publications, Weston Creek ACT, 1995
Fysh, Sir Hudson, *QANTAS at War*, Angus and Robertson, Sydney, 1968
Fysh, Sir Hudson, *Wings to the World*, Angus and Robertson, Sydney, 1970
Gunn, John, *Challenging Horizons*, University of Queensland Press, St Lucia, Queensland, 1987
Gunn, John, *Defeat of Distance*, University of Queensland Press, St Lucia, Queensland, 1985
Gunn, John, *High Corridors*, University of Queensland Press, St Lucia, Queensland, 1988
Hall, Timothy, *Flying High*, Methuen of Australia, Sydney, 1979
Jackson, A.J., *British Civil Aircraft 1919-59 Vol 2*, Putnam, London, 1960
Jackson, Robert, *The Sky Their Frontier*, Arco Publishing Inc, New York, 1984
London, Peter, *British Flying Boats*, Sutton Publishing, Stroud, Gloucestershire, 2003
Lowe, David, *The Flying-Boat Era,* The Lodestar Press, Auckland, 1978
Ludlow, Peter, *Moreton Bay Letters*, Peter Ludlow, Stone's Corner, Qld, 2003
Ludlow, Peter, *Moreton Bay People - Volume IV*, Peter Ludlow, Stone's Corner, Qld, 1996
Marshall, David, & Harris, Bruce, *Dreamers, Doers, & Daredevils*, Five Mile Press, Rowville Victoria, 2003

Miller, H.C., *Early Birds*, Seal Books, Rigby Ltd, Adelaide, 1976
Monkton, Bryan, *The Boats I Flew*, Australian Aviation Museum, Bankstown, 2005
Morison, Samuel Eliot, *New Guinea and the Marianas, March 1944 - August 1944, History of United States Naval Operations in World War II, Vol.8*, Little, Brown & Co, Boston, 1953
Parnell, Neville, & Boughton, Trevor, *Flypast*, Australian Government Publishing Service, Canberra, 1988
Parnell, N.M., & Lynch, C.A., *Australian Air Force since 1911*, J.W. Books Pty Ltd, Brookvale, NSW, 1982
Pentland, Geoffrey, & Malone, Peter, *Aircraft of the RAAF 1921-71*, Kookaburra Technical Publications, Melbourne, 1971
Qantas Empire Airways, *Milestones 1920-1949*, Qantas Empire Airways Ltd, c.1950
Riddell, Jack, *Catalina Squadrons, First and Furthest*, Murwillumbah Print Spot, Murwillumbah NSW, 1997
Sinclair, James, *Wings of Gold*, Robert Brown, Bathurst, NSW, 1983
Stackhouse, John, *...from the dawn of aviation*, Focus Publishing Pty Ltd, Double Bay, NSW, 1995
Stackhouse, John, *The Longest Hop*, Focus Publishing Pty Ltd, Edgecliff, NSW, 1997
Taylor, Sir Gordon, *The Sky Beyond*, Cassell Australia, Melbourne, 1963
Taylor, Sir Gordon, *Bird of the Islands*, Cassell Australia, Melbourne, 1964
Thetford, Owen, *Aircraft of the Royal Air Force 1918-57*, Putnam, London, 1957
Wilson, John, *History of Civil Flying Boat Operations 1946-1974*, John Wilson, Wynnum West, Qld, 1998
Wilson, Stewart, *Catalina, Neptune and Orion in Australian Service*, Aerospace Publications, Weston Creek ACT, 1991
Wilson, Stewart, *Anson, Hudson & Sunderland in Australian Service*, Aerospace Publications, Weston Creek ACT, 1992
Winchester, Clarence (editor), *Wonders of World Aviation, Vol. 2*, The Fleetway House, London, c.1938
Wixted, Edward P., *The North-West Aerial Frontier 1919-1934*, Boolarong Publications, Brisbane, 1985

Articles:

Bartlett, Norman, "By Air to the Reef", *South West Pacific Magazine*, New Series No.18, Dept. of Information, 1947 (John Oxley Library collection VF 387.7 bar)
"The Qantas Fleet List", *AHSA Journal*, vol.10, no.6, Nov-Dec 1970
"Monthly Notes – Civil", *AHSA Journal*, vol.13, no.6, Jan-Feb 1973
Eyre, D.C., "Catalinas on the Great Barrier Reef", *AHSA Journal*, vol.14, no.4, Sep-Oct 1973
Eyre, D.C., "Catalinas in Civil Service", *AHSA Journal*, vol.14, no.6, Jan-Feb 1974
"Monthly Notes – Civil", *AHSA Journal*, vol.15, no.1, Mar-Apr 1974
Eyre, D.C., "*Frigate Bird I & II*", *AHSA Journal*, vol.15, no.2, May-Jun 1974
Eyre, D.C., "Grumman Amphibians in Australia", *AHSA Journal*, vol.15, no.4, Sep-Oct 1974
"Monthly Notes – Civil", *AHSA Journal*, vol.15, no.5, Nov-Dec 1974
"Douglas Commercial Log", *AHSA Journal*, vol.17, no.1, 1976
Croker, M.T., "Trans Oceanic Airways Pty Ltd", *Aviation Heritage*, vol.23, no.1, 1983

Banfield, Greg, "The Stewart Middlemiss Story", *Aviation Heritage*, vol.25, nos.1 & 2, 1987

Department of Harbours and Marine, (Queensland), Annual Reports, y/e 30 June 1946 to y/e 30 June 1954

Department of Transport, (Queensland), Annual Reports, y/e 30 June 1948 to y/e 30 June 1960

Goodall, Geoff, "*Star of Papua*", *Australian Flying*, May-Jun 1982

Goodall, Geoff, "Barrier Reef Mallards", *Australian Flying*, Nov-Dec 1984

Ricketts, Peter, "Flying Boats Return", *Australian Flying*, Nov-Dec 1984

Allen, Eric, "The Short Flying Boats", *Australian Aviation*, Sep 1982

Allen, Eric, "The Consolidated Catalina", *Australian Aviation*, June 1983

"Qantas", *Airplane* vol.2, no.19, Orbis Publishing Ltd, London, 1991-93

"Sandringham Services Increase", *Qantas News*, No.5, May 1953

Newspapers:

The Courier Mail: various issues including

6-7 & 13 August 1925, 11-20 August 1928, 20-24 August 1928, 29 September 1934, 2-6 October 1934, 20-26 May 1936, 22-24 December 1937, 21-28 January 1938, 4-6 April 1938, 4 May 1938, 10 & 27 June 1938, 5-6 July 1938, 5 August 1938, 19 April 1940, 9 December 1941, 10 & 18 May 1946, 1-4 July 1950, 30 October 1950, 4-5 & 21 April 1951, 25-28 May 1951, 16-19 June 1951, 29 October 1951, 11 July 1952, 12 July 1952, 31 October 1952, 1-5 November 1952, 14-15 & 23 January 1953, 28 May 1953, 17 July 1962, 26 January 1963, 13 September 1965, & 16 June 1983.

The Sunday Mail: various issues including

12-19 August 1928, 3 April 1938, 12 September 1965, 13 July 1952, 2 November 1952, & 20 July 1969.

The Telegraph: various issues including

2 July 1947, & 15 June 1983

Video:

From Sea to Sky, Film Affaires P/L, 2005

Oral histories:

McCollum, Rear Admiral A.H. Transcript of interview with J.T. Mason (1971), United States Naval Institute, Annapolis, Maryland

Internet Sites:

www.adastron.com/squawkid/

www.ansett.com.au/administrator/ansettatach1/milestones.pdf

www.daveswarbirds.com/blackcat/

www.hazegray.org/danfs/

www.redland.qld.gov.au/emplibrary/

Index

About the Author

David Jones is a lifelong resident of Brisbane with a keen interest in local history, particularly nautical and aviation history in the Brisbane area. Married with two adult children he retired in 2000 after a career in the Queensland Public Service. Retirement has allowed him more time to pursue his long-standing fascination with aeronautical and maritime history – two areas of interest which found a happy combination in *Wings on the River*. David is a member of the Queensland Maritime Museum and the Queensland Air Museum. His previously books include *U.S. Subs Down Under: Brisbane, 1942-1945* which he co-authored with Peter Nunan, and *The Whalers of Tangalooma*. He has also written several historical papers published in specialist journals.